GOD'S TOUGH LOVE

A study guide through the Minor Prophets

Scott Franks

Scott Garret Publishing

ISBN-13: 978-1491295892
ISBN-10: 1491295899

HOW TO USE THIS GUIDE

Many Christians are almost entirely illiterate when it comes to the prophets because this is not easy material. It includes rich literature, complex poetry, social editorial and fiery sermon. It requires some understanding of the socio-political and religious landscape of a time and place very foreign to us. Yet the applications for modern Christianity, our churches, and our society are startling to say the least.

This book is not meant to be a commentary. This is a study guide that attempts to provide a working understanding of the Minor Prophets, one prophet per lesson, written to fit a typical one-hour class or small group study.

In my experience, most groups prefer a discussion format over a lecture format, and most teachers' shortcoming is knowing how to ask questions that foster discussion. I have attempted to provide you open-ended questions that will draw out discussion, and then in the bullet points after each discussion question, provide some key points or applications that should hopefully come out of the discussion. When a question is subjective, or based on the personal experiences of your group, there are no bullet points because there are no specific "right" answers.

I concentrated these lesson plans on passages that seemed to have the most obvious applications to modern Christians. Our goal is to portray these prophets as vital and living voices within their society (and ours) and rewarding portraits of God's love. A whole series could be done on the Messianic components of the Minor Prophets. While I do occasionally highlight some of these, I did not attempt to point out each and every one.

May God bless you as you open His Word and the eyes of His people.

-Scott Franks December 2013

CONTENTS

SOURCES

Opening the Windows of Blessing from the New Inductive Study Series. Kay Arthur, Pete DeLacy, and Bob Vereen. Harvest House Publishers, 2003. see www.precept.org

Taking God Seriously by Stuart Briscoe. Word Books, 1986. (out of print)

New Bible commentary : 21st century edition. Carson, D. A. 1994. Rev. ed. of: The new Bible commentary. 3rd ed. / edited by D. Guthrie, J.A. Motyer. 1970. (4th ed.) . Inter-Varsity Press: Leicester, England; Downers Grove, Ill., USA

Culver, R. D. (1999). 1277 אָבַן. In R. L. Harris, G. L. Archer, Jr. & B. K. Waltke (Eds.), Theological Wordbook of the Old Testament (R. L. Harris, G. L. Archer, Jr. & B. K. Waltke, Ed.) (electronic ed.) (544). Chicago: Moody Press.

Baker encyclopedia of the Bible. Elwell, W. A., & Beitzel, B. J. 1988. Baker Book House: Grand Rapids, Mich.

Who's Who in the Bible, edited by Paul D. Gardner. Zondervan, 1995.

John Mark Hicks in *The Theology of the Lord's Prayer* on www.johnmarkhicks.faithsite.com

The Minor Prophets by Hampton Keathley on www.bible.org.

Judson Mather, "*The Comic Act of the Book of Jonah,*" *Soundings* 65. Fall 1982, p. 283

Shepherd's Notes – Haggai, Zechariah and Malachi by Barry E. Morgan, Broadman & Holman Publishers, 1999.

Myers, A. C. (1987). *The Eerdmans Bible dictionary (305). Grand Rapids, MI: Eerdmans.*

The teacher's commentary by Richards, L., & Richards, L. O. Victor Books, 1987.

Smith, J. E. (1994). *The Minor Prophets.* Old Testament Survey Series. Joplin, MO: College Press.

Understanding the Bible by John R.W. Stott, Zondervan, 1999.

Interpreting the Prophetic Word by Willem A. VanGemeren. Zondervan, 1990.

My Servants the Prophets Vol. 4 by John T. Willis. Contact ACU Press at www.acu.edu.

1
INTRODUCTION
When a prophet of the lord is among you

To set the stage for interpreting and understanding the minor prophets, we will start by simply defining who was a true prophet and who was not. This was a question with immediate implications in the time of the minor prophets.

<u>Opening Idea:</u> When you hear the words prophet and prophecy, what comes to mind? What mental images or current events do you associate with those words?

Prophet may conjure images of a hairy, scary man tongue-lashing people as they pass on the street. It may have the equally scary cultic connection to modern self-proclaimed and self-destructive "prophets" like Jim Jones or David Koresh. We may associate it with a mystical ability to predict the future.

Who is a prophet?

There are a few words in the Bible that can be translated as *prophet* or that refer to the same sort of person or function. Sometimes that word is *prophet*, sometimes it is *man of God*, and sometimes it is *seer* (*Baker Encyclopedia* 1781). The Hebrew word for prophet – ***nābî*** – could have been derived from an Arabic root meaning "to announce" or "spokesman." It could come from a Hebrew root that meant to "bubble up," hence pour forth words. It might have come from an Akkadian root for "to call" or "one who is called." All of these contain some element of the biblical prophet, but at its most basic, **a *nābî*ʾ is a person authorized to speak for another** (Culver 1277). In the case of the biblical prophets, they were speaking for God. God designated prophets as His unique spokesmen.

Deuteronomy 18:14-20 (NIV)
14 The nations you will dispossess listen to those who practice sorcery or divination. But as for you, the Lord your God has not permitted you to do so. 15 The Lord your God will raise up for you a prophet like me from among you, from your fellow Israelites. You must listen to him. 16 For this is what you asked of the Lord your God at Horeb on the day of the assembly when you said, "Let us not hear the voice of the Lord our God nor see this great fire anymore, or we will die."

The impetus for raising prophets is attributed to the story in Exodus 20 where God audibly spoke the Ten Commandments to the assembled Israelites, and the experience of directly hearing the voice of God was so terrifying that they asked Moses to speak to them on God's behalf instead. Through the prophets, even though they would not be hearing God's voice directly, they were still hearing God.

Napoleon Bonaparte is credited with saying **"The role of a leader is to define reality and then give hope."** We see much the same role in the prophets. They gave the people a realistic assessment of their current (or soon-to-be) situation, but then so often ended with a message of hope.

The prophets brought a reality that was from God's perspective, and at times illuminated how differently God saw things happening among His people. At times the people felt justified by their religious activities, but from God's perspective, those activities were empty rituals and insulting to His holiness. At times the people felt God had abandoned them or no longer cared about justice, but from God's perspective, they were the ones who had abandoned Him.

The prophets made the people see realistically, and that reality could be devastatingly grim, but it was almost always accompanied by hope. The message of hope may have been conditional on their repentance, or it may not have come to fruition until after events predicted by the prophet, but with the promise that because this word came with the authority of God, they would one day know for certain its truth. As God says in **Ezekiel 2:5**, *"And whether they listen or fail to listen – for they are a rebellious people – they will know that a prophet has been among them."*

<u>Group Discussion:</u> How did the prophets receive messages from God? How do you imagine that happened, or what was it like?

a. **Sometimes the prophets described that Spirit experience as being lifted up:** Ezekiel 3:12 (NIV) [12] *Then the Spirit lifted me up, and I heard behind me a loud rumbling sound—May the glory of the Lord be praised in his dwelling place!—*

b. **Or they had a sense that the Spirit had "come upon" them**: Ezekiel 11:5 (NIV) [5] *Then the Spirit of the Lord came upon me, and he told me to say: "This is what the Lord says: That is what you are saying, O house of Israel, but I know what is going through your mind.*

c. **In Numbers, God says that he comes to prophets in dreams and visions**: Numbers 12:6 (NIV) [6] *he said, "Listen to my words: "When a prophet of the Lord is among you, I reveal myself to him in visions, I speak to him in dreams.*

d. **When God first came to Samuel in 1 Samuel 3, it was as a voice in the dark.**

e. **Through the words and person of Jesus**: Hebrews 1:1-2 (NIV) *In the past God spoke to our forefathers through the prophets at many times and in various ways,* [2] *but in these last days he has spoken to us by his Son, whom he appointed heir of all things, and through whom he made the universe.*

However God came to them, we shouldn't view the process of prophecy or inspiration as God using these men and women as robotic dictating machines. Even when the Spirit of God was on them, even when they were prophesying, they were always living, responsible people. Being used by God did not obliterate their personalities. Their literary style and vocabulary were their own. In some of the prophets, we will even see them arguing with God. The bottom line is these were real people, with the same emotions, responsibilities, fears, and faults as all of us (Stott, 159).

Who is not a prophet?

In Hebrew society there was an institution of "professional" prophets who filled an accepted and respected role in government and religion. But sometimes these prophets gave contradictory messages. How could the people determine which prophets were true spokesmen for God? As it says in 1 Thessalonians 5:20-22 (NIV) [20] *Do not treat prophecies with contempt* [21] *but test them all; hold on to what is good,* [22] *reject every kind of evil.*

<u>Group Discussion:</u> Imagine you were an Israelite living in the 7th or 8th century B.C. when many of the minor prophets lived. How would you determine if someone who claimed to be a prophet actually was a true prophet of God? What criteria or tests would you use to validate his message? (make a list on the board, then compare that list to the criteria below)

1. How did he become a prophet?

- The authority to make someone a prophet rests solely with God. Only a false prophet would dare to assume on his own the title of prophet.
- Jeremiah 14:14 (NIV) *14 Then the Lord said to me, "The prophets are prophesying lies in my name. I have not sent them or appointed them or spoken to them. They are prophesying to you false visions, divinations, idolatries and the delusions of their own minds.*
- Amos 7:14-15 (NIV) *14 Amos answered Amaziah, "I was neither a prophet nor the son of a prophet, but I was a shepherd, and I also took care of sycamore-fig trees. 15 But the Lord took me from tending the flock and said to me, 'Go, prophesy to my people Israel.*

2. Do his predictions come true?

- Deuteronomy 18:21-22 (NIV) *21 You may say to yourselves, "How can we know when a message has not been spoken by the Lord?" 22 If what a prophet proclaims in the name of the Lord does not take place or come true, that is a message the Lord has not spoken. That prophet has spoken presumptuously. Do not be afraid of him.*
- **Of course, sometimes that would not work because the prophecy given was not intended to be fulfilled until generations later.**
- Ezekiel 33:33 *"When all this comes true – and it surely will – then they will know that a prophet has been among them."*
- The true prophet proclaimed a historically verifiable message. Unfortunately, the prophets did not always live to see their prophecies fulfilled.

3. Is his message in line with the Mosaic Law and previous messages from God?

- Deuteronomy 13:1-5 (NIV) *If a prophet, or one who foretells by dreams, appears among you and announces to you a miraculous sign or wonder, 2 and if the sign or wonder of which he has spoken takes place, and he says, "Let us follow other gods" (gods you have not known) "and let us worship them," 3 you must not listen to the words of that prophet or dreamer. The Lord your God is testing you to find out whether you love him with all your heart and with all your soul. 4 It is the Lord your God you must follow, and him you must revere. Keep his commands and obey him; serve him and hold fast to him. 5 That prophet or dreamer must be put to death, because he preached rebellion against the Lord your God, who brought you out of Egypt and redeemed you from the land of slavery; he has tried to turn you from the way the Lord your God commanded you to follow. You must purge the evil from among you.*

4. Does he show any sort of special power or equipping by God's Spirit?

- Notice that the previous reading acknowledges that false prophets may have the apparent power to predict signs or interpret dreams, but they are still not true prophets. A "supernatural" talent is not in itself proof for a prophet, but some did have extraordinary powers. Elisha was involved in numerous miracles, from floating an ax head to having clairvoyant gifts of knowing what was said in secret from far away.
- 2 Kings 6:5-12 (NIV) *5 As one of them was cutting down a tree, the iron axhead fell into the water. "Oh no, my lord!" he cried out. "It was borrowed!" 6 The man of God asked, "Where did it fall?" When he showed him the place, Elisha cut a stick and threw it there, and made the iron float. 7 "Lift it out," he said. Then the man reached out his hand and took it. 8 Now the king of Aram was at war with Israel. After conferring with his*

officers, he said, "I will set up my camp in such and such a place." [9] *The man of God sent word to the king of Israel: "Beware of passing that place, because the Arameans are going down there."* [10] *So the king of Israel checked on the place indicated by the man of God. Time and again Elisha warned the king, so that he was on his guard in such places.* [11] *This enraged the king of Aram. He summoned his officers and demanded of them, "Tell me! Which of us is on the side of the king of Israel?"* [12] *"None of us, my lord the king," said one of his officers, "but Elisha, the prophet who is in Israel, tells the king of Israel the very words you speak in your bedroom."*

5. Is there any meat, any challenge in his message?

- Jeremiah 23:25-29 (NIV) [25] *"I have heard what the prophets say who prophesy lies in my name. They say, 'I had a dream! I had a dream!'* [26] *How long will this continue in the hearts of these lying prophets, who prophesy the delusions of their own minds?* [27] *They think the dreams they tell one another will make my people forget my name, just as their fathers forgot my name through Baal worship.* [28] *Let the prophet who has a dream tell his dream, but let the one who has my word speak it faithfully. For what has straw to do with grain?" declares the Lord.* [29] *"Is not my word like fire," declares the Lord, "and like a hammer that breaks a rock in pieces?*
- Micah 2:11 (NIV) [11] *If a liar and deceiver comes and says, 'I will prophesy for you plenty of wine and beer,' he would be just the prophet for this people!*
- God's Word has been described as fire, as a hammer, as a sword. It has a power to challenge and change human hearts. The false prophets' message was compared to straw –empty, cheap filler that does not challenge or offend anyone. Someone once said that genuine Godly preaching afflicts the comfortable and comforts the afflicted.

6. What is in this for him?

- Jeremiah 8:10b-11 (NIV) [10] *From the least to the greatest, all are greedy for gain; prophets and priests alike, all practice deceit.* [11] *They dress the wound of my people as though it were not serious. "Peace, peace," they say, when there is no peace.*
- The false prophets had some sort of ulterior motive. They expected to be liked or rewarded for their message. The true prophet was usually the object of ridicule, hatred and plots. He was often a lonely outcast, and usually at odds with the culture around him. No sane person would choose the true prophets' lifestyle unless he was thoroughly convinced of the truth of his message. For the most part, the prophet was saying exactly what his audience did *not* want to hear.
- Acts 7:52 (NIV) [52] *Was there ever a prophet your fathers did not persecute? They even killed those who predicted the coming of the Righteous One."*

7. Who is he working for?

- It was inevitable that the monarchy would develop a group of professional counselors/prophets to promote the interests of the monarch. False prophets were guardians of the status quo. Their hope was fixed on institutions (the temple, the monarchy) rather than the living God. True prophets generally worked outside any social structure. (VanGemeren 64)
- Notice how the prophets and priests in the following episode treat Jeremiah when he prophecies things that threaten the status quo. They loved their city more than God's word: **Jeremiah 26:8-11** (NIV) [8] *But as soon as Jeremiah finished telling all the people everything the Lord had commanded him to say, the priests, the prophets and all the people seized him and said, "You must die!* [9] *Why do you prophesy in the Lord's name that this house will be like Shiloh and this city will be desolate and deserted?" And all the people crowded around Jeremiah in the house of the Lord.* [10] *When the officials of Judah heard about these things, they went up from the royal palace to the house of the Lord and took their places at the entrance of the New Gate of the Lord's house.* [11] *Then the priests and the prophets said to the officials and all the people, "This man should be sentenced to death because he has prophesied against this city. You have heard it with your own ears!"*

8. How free is his God?

- Perhaps the subtlest yet most important difference between true prophets and false prophets lay in their view of God's freedom. The false prophets called on God, quoted scripture, and were very "religious" in their behavior. They were zealous for the Mosaic Law and all the Hebrew traditions but resistant to any interpretation or new revelation that might alter their understanding of God or Israel. They did not want to listen to God when His message was inconvenient or incongruent with their preconceived (often selfish) notions of Him. To them, God was static and historic (VanGemeren 60).
- The true prophets, by contrast, were open to new revelations. They recognized that God, the Creator of everything, was free to rule over His creation. That freedom included allowing foreign nations to carry off His people as punishment, or to be generous to both the Israelites and their Gentile neighbors.
- True prophets served God. False prophets used God to serve themselves.

Group Discussion: Have you seen anything in our discussion of the prophets so far that is still relevant today? Were there any issues in the time of the prophets that are again issues in our churches or society today?

Group Discussion: In our discussion of how the people had to discern between true and false prophets, have you seen any practical applications for us as the modern People of God?

- Do we just want to be fed "feel-good filler?" Do we avoid being challenged and punish teachers that do challenge us to change?
- Are we defenders of the status quo more dedicated to Godly institutions than to God Himself?

Group Discussion If you are a Christian, what role does Old Testament prophecy play in your daily life, if any? Have you found any application for these books?

It may be hard to see any connection between us and the obscure books at the end of the Old Testament. They talk about nations and kings that are now no more than dust. They predict a Messiah that has already come. They practice a religious system of animal sacrifices that looks nothing like what we do in our churches. Why bother?

We hope that the relevance of this study will become clear to you soon. For the next few months, we are going to open a book in your Bible that you've probably never heard of: The Book of the Twelve. This was what the Hebrews in Jesus' time would have called the last twelve books in our Old Testament. We now call them the Minor Prophets. It's no reflection on their importance, but simply because what they wrote was shorter than the "major" prophets.

Obadiah, Habakkuk, Haggai . . . Not exactly household names, are they? Except for Jonah, most people don't know much at all about these men or the books they wrote. Yet these men were essential to the message of God to His people then and now. God spoke through these men. They expressed God's anger, God's love, and God's plans, so through their writings, we see the personality of our God.

2
HOSEA
God does not love like man

Preaching to a comfortable corpse (historical context)

Hosea 1:1 (NIV)

The word of the Lord that came to Hosea son of Beeri during the reigns of Uzziah, Jotham, Ahaz and Hezekiah, kings of Judah, and during the reign of Jeroboam son of Jehoash king of Israel:

Hosea lived during a time when the original Twelve Tribes of Israel were divided into two kingdoms: the northern kingdom of Israel (also called Ephraim in this book) and the southern kingdom of Judah. He was one of the last prophets to the northern kingdom, although it's possible he also lived and preached in Judah at some point. He lived during a time of national prosperity that was almost as great as the "golden age" of David and Solomon. But the wealth was not distributed fairly. The rich and powerful grew ever richer while the farmers and working class suffered poverty and oppression. The ruling class in Israel was especially corrupt. Several kings came to the throne by assassinating their predecessors, only to be killed in later coups. Israel's monarchs were involved in numerous alliances with foreign powers for the sake of survival, and these treaties eventually caused their destruction by the Assyrian Empire. Israel was rich but rotting from within.

The religious context in which Hosea prophesied is reflected in many parts of the book. The Israelites under Joshua had conquered the land of Canaan but had failed to destroy the peoples already settled there. They and their descendants, and their religion, continued. The Canaanites worshipped many gods, the chief of which was called Baal. Baal was supposed to be the god who gave fertility to the land. According to myth he was killed by Moth, the god of summer and drought, but rose from the dead after the goddess Anath avenged his murder. This dying and rising reflected the annual cycle of the seasons. Canaanite religion was designed to give fertility to the land; it did not place a high value on morals. At the temples, men were able to 'worship' Baal and stimulate him to acts of fertility by having sexual intercourse with 'sacred' resident prostitutes.

Israel was supposed to worship one God, 'the Lord', who could not be manipulated by ritual but required strict obedience instead. Clearly, the two religions were incompatible, but the Israelites tried to mix them anyway (Carson, New Bible commentary on 1 Ki. 18:21).

The religious decline of Israel is summed up this way by God through Hosea:
Hosea 13:4-6 (NIV)
4 *"But I am the Lord your God,*
who brought you out of Egypt.
You shall acknowledge no God but me,
no Savior except me.
5 *I cared for you in the desert,*
in the land of burning heat.
6 *When I fed them, they were satisfied;*
when they were satisfied, they became proud;
then they forgot me.

Israel no longer had the distinctiveness of being a counterculture shaped by divine revelation. They looked and acted like everyone else and became complacent with God. Hosea preached to people who still enjoyed the benefits of an economic boom and a historical identity as God's people, but who were about to experience major national crises in rapid succession. To get their attention, to illustrate the shock treatment He was about to use on Israel, God asked Hosea to do something shocking.

A marriage made in heaven?

Hosea 1:2-9 (NIV)
2 *When the Lord began to speak through Hosea, the Lord said to him, "Go, take to yourself an adulterous wife and children of unfaithfulness, because the land is guilty of the vilest adultery in departing from the Lord ."*
3 *So he married Gomer daughter of Diblaim, and she conceived and bore him a son.*
4 *Then the Lord said to Hosea, "Call him Jezreel, because I will soon punish the house of Jehu for the massacre at Jezreel, and I will put an end to the kingdom of Israel.*
5 *In that day I will break Israel's bow in the Valley of Jezreel."*
6 *Gomer conceived again and gave birth to a daughter. Then the Lord said to Hosea, "Call her Lo-Ruhamah, for I will no longer show love to the house of Israel, that I should at all forgive them.*
7 *Yet I will show love to the house of Judah; and I will save them—not by bow, sword or battle, or by horses and horsemen, but by the Lord their God."*
8 *After she had weaned Lo-Ruhamah, Gomer had another son.*
9 *Then the Lord said, "Call him Lo-Ammi, for you are not my people, and I am not your God.*

<u>Group Discussion</u>: What are the interpretations of the names of Hosea's children? What is the significance or message in each of those names?

- Jezreel means "God sows" or "God scatters." In this instance, the negative connotation was intended. As a place name, Jezreel was also symbolic of bloodshed because Jezreel was a plain where many battles were fought, and the homeplace of a vineyard owner treacherously killed by the wicked queen Jezebel.
- Lo-Ruhamah means "not loved" or "not pitied." God is telling Israel they cannot take for granted his love and protection.
- Lo-Ammi means "not my people." This is a final rejection that jerks away from Israel their special standing as God's chosen people. Basically, God is saying that Israel can assume nothing now.

While it appears that Jezreel was the biological son of Hosea, there is a possibility, based on the allusion to "children of unfaithfulness" in 1:2, and an allegory in Hosea 2:4-5, that the last two kids were the result of adulterous affairs, and were not his.

Hosea 2:4-5 (NIV)
4 I will not show my love to her children, because they are the children of adultery.
5 Their mother has been unfaithful and has conceived them in disgrace.
She said, 'I will go after my lovers, who give me my food and my water,
my wool and my linen, my oil and my drink.'

Imagine the dynamic in this family. The three kids are named God scatters, Not Loved, and Not My People. Two of them are probably illegitimate. Gomer is an unfaithful wife, and perhaps even a prostitute. Based on the traditional time period for weaning children in those days, it is possible that these three kids were born over a period of ten years.

Group Discussion: How could you see all this affecting God's prophet Hosea in his home life, his faith, and in the effectiveness of his preaching?

- People would wonder how a true man of God could have such a sad family.
- Hosea would have to wonder why God would "mess" with his family like this. Hosea and his family are being "used" by God in the worst way – as an object lesson that illustrates in living color spiritual adultery. Yet this family is composed of real people who would feel deeply and personally the scorn of their neighbors. God seems to have doomed Hosea's entire family to failure. This would be a heartbreaking test of faith.

Group Discussion: If you were Hosea, what would your prayers be like?

Making up is hard to do

In chapter 3 of Hosea, the story of this "marriage made in heaven" is picked up again. It appears that Gomer has entirely left her family and is now a working prostitute. Hosea is given another command from God concerning his wife:

Hosea 3:1-5 (NIV)
The Lord said to me, "Go, show your love to your wife again, though she is loved by another and is an adulteress. Love her as the Lord loves the Israelites, though they turn to other gods and love the sacred raisin cakes."
2 So I bought her for fifteen shekels of silver and about a homer and a lethek of barley. 3 Then I told her, "You are to live with me many days; you must not be a prostitute or be intimate with any man, and I will live with you."
4 For the Israelites will live many days without king or prince, without sacrifice or sacred stones, without ephod or idol. 5
Afterward the Israelites will return and seek the Lord their God and David their king. They will come trembling to the Lord and to his blessings in the last days.

The price he pays for her – fifteen shekels – is significant. Remember how much the traitor Judas received for Jesus? It was thirty pieces of silver. Thirty pieces of silver was the price of a slave. Fifteen shekels was the value of a slave at half-price – the price reflected that this slave was "damaged goods" (Briscoe 19).

Group Discussion: What would you advise Hosea to do if you were his friend? He entered into a doomed marriage because he thought that is what God wanted, and then when he is finally free of this horribly draining woman, he tells you he is going to go find her again - this adulterous embarrassment who had left him with three kids. Hosea will have to pay off her debts, and then live with her in an arrangement something like house arrest for a sex addict. If Hosea told you this was his plan, what would your advice be to him?

So with all those valid reasons for not wasting time on this lost cause, why is God sending Hosea to find Gomer yet again? The answer is in Hosea 11:8-9,

Hosea 11:8-9 (NIV)
8 "How can I give you up, Ephraim? How can I hand you over, Israel? How can I treat you like Admah? How can I make you like Zeboiim? My heart is changed within me; all my compassion is aroused.
9 I will not carry out my fierce anger, nor will I turn and devastate Ephraim. For I am God, and not man— the Holy One among you. I will not come in wrath.

Admah and Zeboiim were villages near Sodom destroyed by God when He wiped out Sodom and Gomorrah.

Group Discussion: When He says "I am God and not man," what point is God making with that comparison?

- In human terms, Hosea's redemption of Gomer made no sense. But God loves differently than we do. God, unlike man, is Holy. His love for us is holy and His patience far exceeds humans. God loves the unlovable like no one else can.
- God's love is complete and perfect, and can heal everything in our past. It is the kind of love mentioned in **1 Peter 4:8** (NIV): 8 Above all, love each other deeply, because love covers over a multitude of sins.

Group Discussion: In looking at God's commands to Hosea in chapters 1 and 3, what are God's priorities?

Once more, with feeling . . .

Repentance is a major theme of many prophets, including Hosea. Read again Hosea 3. Then read Hosea 6:1-6 and 7:14.

Hosea 6:1-6 (NIV)
"Come, let us return to the Lord. He has torn us to pieces but he will heal us; he has injured us but he will bind up our wounds.
2 After two days he will revive us; on the third day he will restore us, that we may live in his presence.
3 Let us acknowledge the Lord; let us press on to acknowledge him.
As surely as the sun rises, he will appear; he will come to us like the winter rains, like the spring rains that water the earth."
4 "What can I do with you, Ephraim? What can I do with you, Judah? Your love is like the morning mist, like the early dew that disappears.
5 Therefore I cut you in pieces with my prophets, I killed you with the words of my mouth; my judgments flashed like lightning upon you.
6 For I desire mercy, not sacrifice, and acknowledgment of God rather than burnt offerings.

Hosea 7:14 (NIV)
14 They do not cry out to me from their hearts
but wail upon their beds.
They gather together for grain and new wine
but turn away from me.

<u>Group Discussion:</u> What does God expect in true repentance?

- Humility – "they will come trembling"
- A change in behavior, not just a change in words. God wants service, not just lip service.
- Sorrow over sin and separation from God, not sorrow over "getting caught" or self-sorrow because of the discipline we are now receiving from our Father.
- A willingness to pay our dues and wait on God. In Hosea 6 the people are chided for treating God's forgiveness and His blessings as if they came from a tap. If they simply recited the right words, they expected immediate reconciliation and gratification. Then they would soon drift back to their preferred selfishness. Many times, though, God works on us over time. It is not until Israel reached bottom, until it was a decimated, exiled people, that it came back to God.

When we hear the story of this bizarre marriage, we put ourselves in Hosea's shoes and conclude that this makes no sense. If this is love, it makes no sense. But that story is not told for us to identify with Hosea. We're not Hosea, we're Gomer! We are the hopeless sinners addicted to what kills us spiritually. Jesus knew that about us from the beginning. Yet He loved us against all reason, and then paid everything to find us and redeem us until we finally came to our senses and loved him back on his terms.

3
JOEL
The Day of the Lord

We know very little about the person or time period of Joel. He may have lived in Jerusalem since he speaks to Jerusalem and Judah. He doesn't associate himself with a particular king, and nothing in his writings allows scholars to pinpoint when he lived. These unknowns do not detract from his message.

Laid Low

Joel writes his prophecy after three inter-related natural disasters have hit the land:

1. **Locusts** (Joel 1:4, 6-7)
2. **Drought** (Joel 1:12, 16-18)
3. **Wildfire** (Joel 1:19-20)

The locusts are referred to by four different descriptions in Joel 1:4 and 2:25: the great locusts, the young locusts, the other locusts, and the locust swarm. The precise meaning of the four Hebrew words used here for locusts is uncertain. It could refer to developmental stages in the life cycle of locusts, or to different species of locusts that have flown through (NIV Study Bible notes for Joel 1:4 and 2:25).

Locusts symbolized powerful and merciless enemies that completely destroyed the earnings of human toil (Jgs 6:5; Is 33:4; Jer 46:23; 51:27; Na 3:15). Masses of them form a random procession of overflowing locust bodies which ignore any obstruction. The only regulator of their activities is temperature; they are immobilized by high or low temperatures. Taking to wing they may move 1,200 miles from their native home. They fly in compact formations large enough to blot out the light of the sun. Their movement seems to be controlled by hormones, but the direction is influenced by the wind. Locusts are still a serious problem, particularly in east Africa. A desert locust swarm can cover 460 square miles and pack 40-80 million locusts into less than half a square mile. (see "Locust," *National Geographic*, http://animals.nationalgeographic.com/animals/bugs/locusts/).

There's a Great Day Coming

For Joel, the locust plague served as a metaphor for the Day of the Lord, a time of revenge and judgment. As bad as the locust plague was, the Day of the Lord would be far worse. The locusts were a judgment from God for his people's sins. But, if the people sincerely repented before God, He would again bless them and pour out His Spirit and protection on them.

There are three parts to Joel's prophecy, and these are related - sometimes as cause/effect - to each other (VanGemeren 121).

Outline of Joel		
Catastrophe of the locust plague (2:1-11)	Is a sign of:	An even greater calamity on the Day of the Lord (3:1-16)
Lament of the locust plague (1:2-20)	Turns into:	Joy as they receive God's blessings (2:18-27)
Call to repent (2:12-17)	Will bring:	Outpouring of the Spirit (2:28-32)

The first clear connection between what was happening with the locusts and what it signaled is seen in Joel 1:15 (NIV)
15 Alas for that day! For the day of the Lord is near; it will come like destruction from the Almighty.

In verse 15, Joel clearly links the dreadful days following the locust plague with the "Day of the Lord." He wants the people to recognize in this natural disaster the work of God as judgment, and also a preview of what God's judgment will be for all people and nations.

***The Day of the Lord* is a phrase used by several Old Testament prophets. This term speaks particularly of war. It is an idiom that was used in other ancient Near Eastern cultures. When they said "The Day of the Lord," they understood that to mean war. (Gardner 349).**

That might help explain what we'll read next in Joel chapter 2, where Joel describes an invading army coming on "the Day of the Lord."

Joel 2:1-11 (NIV)
Blow the trumpet in Zion; sound the alarm on my holy hill. Let all who live in the land tremble, for the day of the Lord is coming. It is close at hand—
2 *a day of darkness and gloom, a day of clouds and blackness. Like dawn spreading across the mountains a large and mighty army comes, such as never was of old nor ever will be in ages to come.*
3 *Before them fire devours, behind them a flame blazes. Before them the land is like the garden of Eden, behind them, a desert waste— nothing escapes them.*
4 *They have the appearance of horses; they gallop along like cavalry.*
5 *With a noise like that of chariots they leap over the mountaintops, like a crackling fire consuming stubble, like a mighty army drawn up for battle.*
6 *At the sight of them, nations are in anguish; every face turns pale.*
7 *They charge like warriors; they scale walls like soldiers. They all march in line, not swerving from their course.*
8 *They do not jostle each other; each marches straight ahead. They plunge through defenses without breaking ranks.*
9 *They rush upon the city; they run along the wall. They climb into the houses; like thieves they enter through the windows.*
10 *Before them the earth shakes, the sky trembles, the sun and moon are darkened, and the stars no longer shine.*
11 *The Lord thunders at the head of his army; his forces are beyond number, and mighty are those who obey his command. The day of the Lord is great; it is dreadful. Who can endure it?*

Some commentators believe this is describing an actual army that will eventually invade Judah, so the locusts are a harbinger of that coming army. Others see this as just another poetical description of the locusts because this seems to describe the movement of locusts well (they leap over mountains, like thieves they enter through the windows, etc.), and also because Joel refers to the locusts as a devouring army in 2:25.

Let's look at some of the other occurrences of this phrase "Day of the Lord." Pay attention to common themes, images, or messages in these scriptures.

Isaiah 13:4-13 (NIV)

4 Listen, a noise on the mountains, like that of a great multitude! Listen, an uproar among the kingdoms, like nations massing together! The Lord Almighty is mustering an army for war.
5 They come from faraway lands, from the ends of the heavens— the Lord and the weapons of his wrath— to destroy the whole country.
6 Wail, for the day of the Lord is near; it will come like destruction from the Almighty.
7 Because of this, all hands will go limp, every man's heart will melt.
8 Terror will seize them, pain and anguish will grip them; they will writhe like a woman in labor. They will look aghast at each other, their faces aflame.
9 See, the day of the Lord is coming —a cruel day, with wrath and fierce anger— to make the land desolate and destroy the sinners within it.
10 The stars of heaven and their constellations will not show their light. The rising sun will be darkened and the moon will not give its light.
11 I will punish the world for its evil, the wicked for their sins. I will put an end to the arrogance of the haughty and will humble the pride of the ruthless.
12 I will make man scarcer than pure gold, more rare than the gold of Ophir.
13 Therefore I will make the heavens tremble; and the earth will shake from its place at the wrath of the Lord Almighty, in the day of his burning anger.

Amos 5:18-20 (NIV)

18 Woe to you who long for the day of the Lord! Why do you long for the day of the Lord? That day will be darkness, not light.
19 It will be as though a man fled from a lion only to meet a bear, as though he entered his house and rested his hand on the wall only to have a snake bite him.
20 Will not the day of the Lord be darkness, not light— pitch-dark, without a ray of brightness?

Zepheniah 1:14-18 (NIV)

14 *The great day of the Lord is near— near and coming quickly. The cry on the day of the Lord is bitter; the Mighty Warrior shouts his battle cry.*
15 *That day will be a day of wrath— a day of distress and anguish, a day of trouble and ruin, a day of darkness and gloom, a day of clouds and blackness—*
16 *a day of trumpet and battle cry against the fortified cities and against the corner towers.*
17 *"I will bring such distress on all people that they will grope about like those who are blind,*
because they have sinned against the Lord. Their blood will be poured out like dust and their entrails like dung.
18 *Neither their silver nor their gold will be able to save them on the day of the Lord's wrath."*
In the fire of his jealousy the whole earth will be consumed, for he will make a sudden end of all who live on the earth.

Obadiah 15 (NIV)

15 "The day of the Lord is near for all nations. As you have done, it will be done to you; your deeds will return upon your own head.

Group Discussion: What recurring images, what themes, what messages do you see in these references?

- Common images include darkness, destruction, noise and fear.
  - Did you notice how a wave of locusts could suggest an apocalyptic Day of the Lord? Clouds of approaching locusts could block out the sun. Joel describes the noise of their destruction, much like an uncountable army.

- Also notice how The Day of the Lord is inescapable and insurmountable. The locusts go everywhere, just like God's knowledge and judgment.

- The prophets tell God's wayward people: "Be afraid. Be very afraid." It is that fear that may compel them to repentance.
- There is also some hopeful promises. In that Day, God comes to defend His people and revenge their enemies. Justice will finally be served.
- It is the Lord's Day, meaning He is in control. He says "I will do this." There is no question who has ultimate authority.

Group Discussion: Joel sees a direct connection between this natural disaster and divine judgment. In fact, he says of the locusts, "The Lord thunders at the head of his army (2:11)." Is every natural catastrophe either God punishing us for sin, or a reminder of the ultimate disastrous Day of Judgment? To what extent would you feel comfortable applying Joel's warnings to a modern natural disaster?

- While it is true that God has shown his wrath through natural phenomena, and that He has uses floods and fires and droughts as punishments in the Bible, it is dangerous for us to correlate one disaster with a particular event in culture or government. God is always displeased by sin, but does not always respond with a natural disaster. In the most terrible of disasters and storms, there are always inspiring stories of faith. God can use such events for many purposes simultaneously – as a warning, as an opportunity for ministry, as a punishment, etc. – so it is beyond our ability to identify a moral judgment as the singular cause of something like a hurricane.
- Jesus teaches in Luke that while we cannot correlate moral reasons to every fatality in a disaster, we can know that what God has said all through scripture about ultimate judgment holds true. All we can do is be sure that individually, we are ready for that day, whenever it may come for us.
  - Luke 13:1-5 (NIV) *Now there were some present at that time who told Jesus about the Galileans whose blood Pilate had mixed with their sacrifices. 2 Jesus answered, "Do you think that these Galileans were worse sinners than all the other Galileans because they suffered this way? 3 I tell you, no! But unless you repent, you too will all perish. 4 Or those eighteen who died when the tower in Siloam fell on them—do you think they were more guilty than all the others living in Jerusalem? 5 I tell you, no! But unless you repent, you too will all perish."*

Rend your heart, not your garments

In response to the current natural disaster and the coming "Day of the Lord," Joel instructs the people to sound an alarm, declare a fast, and gather in a solemn assembly to pray and weep.

Joel 1:14 (NIV)
14 Declare a holy fast; call a sacred assembly.
Summon the elders and all who live in the land
to the house of the Lord your God, and cry out to the Lord.

Joel 2:12 (NIV)
12 'Even now,' declares the Lord,
'return to me with all your heart,
with fasting and weeping and mourning.'

<u>Group Discussion:</u> **What does a fast signify, or what would be accomplished by fasting?**

- It is a reminder of their dependence on God
- It is a way to be still, cease from other normal activity, and "listen" to God
- It is a sign of repentance and humility.

Then Joel gives some commentary to explain to the people what God wants in very practical terms:

Joel 2:13-14 (NIV)

13 *Rend your heart and not your garments. Return to the Lord your God, for he is gracious and compassionate, slow to anger and abounding in love, and he relents from sending calamity.*

14 *Who knows? He may turn and have pity and leave behind a blessing— grain offerings and drink offerings for the Lord your God.*

<u>Group Discussion:</u> **What does it mean to "rend your heart and not your garments?"**

- The custom of tearing one's clothes was part of the cultural reaction to crisis, which still survives in the Jewish practice of tearing the jacket lapel at a funeral (Carson, *New Bible Commentary* on 2 Kings 19:1)
- Such a serious situation – the locusts and the coming judgment – requires a serious response. If they will listen to the alarm, if they will come to the solemn assembly with a serious repentance that is heartfelt and more than just dramatics, their serious response will be the very basis of blessing (Briscoe 35).

<u>Group Discussion:</u> **In our culture, tearing clothes is not how we show repentance or grief. Put this last passage into modern context. What are some ways we "show" repentance in our modern Christian context, and how can we be certain that change of heart is not just "show?"**

- *The Message* paraphrases Joel 2:13 this way: "Change your life, not just your clothes."

Joel begins a new section in 2:18. It describes God's answer to His people's repentance. This could either be past tense (Then the Lord *was* jealous and took pity) or future tense (The Lord *will be* jealous and take pity). It is unclear if it is something that did happen or will happen, but it describes a time of healing and restoration after the disasters of the locusts and drought and fire:

Joel 2:18-27 (NIV)

18 *Then the Lord was jealous for his land and took pity on his people.*
19 *The Lord replied to them:*
"I am sending you grain, new wine and olive oil,
enough to satisfy you fully; never again will I make you
an object of scorn to the nations.
20 *"I will drive the northern horde far from you,*
pushing it into a parched and barren land;
its eastern ranks will drown in the Dead Sea
and its western ranks in the Mediterranean Sea.
And its stench will go up; its smell will rise."

Locusts are a source of pestilence because of the putrefaction of their accumulated bodies. Their excrement could be smelled 150 miles away (*Baker Encyclopedia of the Bible).*

Surely he has done great things!
21 *Do not be afraid, land of Judah;*

be glad and rejoice.
Surely the Lord has done great things!
22 *Do not be afraid, you wild animals,*
for the pastures in the wilderness are becoming green.
The trees are bearing their fruit;
the fig tree and the vine yield their riches.
23 *Be glad, people of Zion,*
rejoice in the Lord your God,
for he has given you the autumn rains
because he is faithful.
He sends you abundant showers,
both autumn and spring rains, as before.
24 *The threshing floors will be filled with grain;*
the vats will overflow with new wine and oil.
25 *"I will repay you for the years the locusts have eaten—*
the great locust and the young locust,
the other locusts and the locust swarm—
my great army that I sent among you.
26 *You will have plenty to eat, until you are full,*
and you will praise the name of the Lord your God,
who has worked wonders for you;
never again will my people be shamed.
27 *Then you will know that I am in Israel,*
that I am the Lord your God,
and that there is no other;
never again will my people be shamed.

After this jubilant outpouring of blessing and restoration for Judah, Joel prophecies about another, future Day of the Lord that will include many more people.

Joel 2:28-32 (NIV)
28 *"And afterward,*
I will pour out my Spirit on all people.
Your sons and daughters will prophesy,
your old men will dream dreams,
your young men will see visions.
29 *Even on my servants, both men and women,*
I will pour out my Spirit in those days.
30 *I will show wonders in the heavens*
and on the earth,
blood and fire and billows of smoke.
31 *The sun will be turned to darkness*
and the moon to blood
before the coming of the great and dreadful day of the Lord.
32 *And everyone who calls*
on the name of the Lord will be saved;
for on Mount Zion and in Jerusalem
there will be deliverance,

as the Lord has said,
even among the survivors whom the Lord calls.

<u>Group Discussion:</u> Did that passage sound familiar? Where else does it appear in the Bible?

- This is quoted by Peter on the day of Pentecost in Acts 2, which is the only other mention of Joel by name elsewhere in scripture.

<u>Group Discussion:</u> Why would Peter see the events of Acts 2 as fulfillment of this prophecy?

- "I will pour out my Spirit" with wonders is exactly what happened on Pentecost, as promised by Christ in Acts 1:5 and 1:8. Peter is also building in this sermon towards salvation in Christ, which is what Joel said: "And everyone who calls on the name of the Lord will be saved."

<u>Group Discussion:</u> How do you explain the part of the prophecy about the sun going dark and the moon turning to blood? Those things did not actually happen on Pentecost.

- Although the sun did not go dark on Pentecost, many people there would have witnessed the supernatural darkness from noon until 3:00 pm on the day Christ died (Matthew 27:45). That would have been seen as a precursor to this event.
- These celestial signs are also prophetic symbolism to describe a momentous change, an unmistakable shift in history or intervention by God. Things like the moon turning to blood, a darkened sky, or an earthquake were synonymous with acts of cosmic disruption that could only be caused by God. This was symbolically saying that God was intervening in human history, or was acting in judgment. See Isaiah 13:13, Amos 8:8-9, and Revelation 6:12-17 for examples.

Joel's prophecy in 2:28-32, quoted by Peter in Acts 2, is applied elsewhere by Paul and others because it contains a wonderful hope for all people, and in it is a message central to the gospel:

Romans 10:11-13 (NIV)

11 *As Scripture says, "Anyone who believes in him will never be put to shame."* 12 *For there is no difference between Jew and Gentile—the same Lord is Lord of all and richly blesses all who call on him,* 13 *for, "Everyone who calls on the name of the Lord will be saved."*

Joel 3 is a prophecy, a warning, even a taunt, against Tyre, Sidon, and Philistia, the nations neighboring Judah on the coast of the Mediterranean. God promises that what they have done to His people – sold them into slavery and plundered them – will be turned on them. God challenges them to battle against Him. Of course there would be no such battle, only God's supreme judgment. In this section, there is an idiom that appears elsewhere in the Bible, and is worth a little discussion.

Plowshares into Swords

Joel 3:9-12 (NIV)

9 *Proclaim this among the nations:*
Prepare for war! Rouse the warriors!
Let all the fighting men draw near and attack.
10 *Beat your plowshares into swords and your pruning hooks into spears.*
Let the weakling say, "I am strong!"
11 *Come quickly, all you nations from every side,*
and assemble there.
Bring down your warriors, Lord!

12 *"Let the nations be roused; let them advance into the Valley of Jehoshaphat,*
for there I will sit to judge all the nations on every side.

"Beat your plowshares into swords" is an idiom that may recall the story in 1 Samuel 13:19-23. The Philistines had forbidden blacksmiths among the Israelites so that Israel could not fashion metal weapons that could be used in a rebellion. In preparation for war, the Israelites went to Philistine blacksmiths to sharpen their plowshares, axes and sickles, and later used those tools as weapons.

This phrase appears in two other prophets, though reversed:

Isaiah 2:2-4 (NIV)

2 *In the last days*
the mountain of the Lord's temple will be established
as the highest of the mountains;
it will be exalted above the hills,
and all nations will stream to it.
3 *Many peoples will come and say,*
"Come, let us go up to the mountain of the Lord,
to the temple of the God of Jacob.
He will teach us his ways,
so that we may walk in his paths."
The law will go out from Zion,
the word of the Lord from Jerusalem.
4 *He will judge between the nations*
and will settle disputes for many peoples.
They will beat their swords into plowshares
and their spears into pruning hooks.
Nation will not take up sword against nation,
nor will they train for war anymore.

Micah quotes the passage above from Isaiah, and adds this to the end:

Micah 4:4-5 (NIV)

4 *Everyone will sit under their own vine and under their own fig tree,*
and no one will make them afraid, for the Lord Almighty has spoken.
5 *All the nations may walk in the name of their gods,*
but we will walk in the name of the Lord our God for ever and ever.

Group Discussion: When this phrase is used in describing a time when God is honored and His kingdom or "mountain" is established, then *plowshares to swords* (peace-time tools turned to weapons) reverses to become *swords to plowshares* (weapons into peace-time tools). What is the message in that turn of a phrase?

- It is definitely a message of hope. There will be a time when we will no longer live in fear, when war will no longer be a necessity or part of our experience because we will live in the harmony and safety of God.

Group Discussion: Some people use these verses as proof that Christians should be pacifists. Do you think that is accurate?

- While the Christian influence should indeed bring peace, and that we should work to be peacemakers, it is not necessarily an accurate application of prophecies about a future state to assume that we can live as if that state exists now. There is a movement that argues that the early Christians were pacifists.
- On the other hand, God definitely used war to bring about His purposes, such as in the conquest of Canaan. When soldiers came to John the Baptist in Luke 3:14 to ask what they should do to live obediently, he said, "*Do not extort money from anyone by threats or by false accusation, and be content with your wages.*" He tells them to serve honorably. He does not tell them to drop their spears and refuse any longer to be soldiers.

4
AMOS
Prepare to meet your God!

Background

Susan D

Amos 1:1 (NIV)

The words of Amos, one of the shepherds of Tekoa—what he saw concerning Israel two years before the earthquake, when Uzziah was king of Judah and Jeroboam son of Jehoash was king of Israel.

The name Amos means *burden bearer.* While he calls himself a shepherd (and later in Amos 7:14 adds that he is a "dresser of sycamore fig trees"), he was probably not a peasant. The word interpreted as *shepherd* here is used just one other time in the Old Testament, in 2 Kings 3:4, where it is used to describe Mesha, king of Moab, who was clearly not a peasant sheepherder. Possibly Amos was a successful sheep merchant and orchard owner. (Gardner 39).

The earthquake mentioned by Amos must have been truly cataclysmic because it is remembered even 240 years later by the prophet Zechariah (Zech. 14:5).

Amos is a contemporary of Hosea, so the historical background in that lesson is applicable to this one as well. Israel and Judah are enjoying a time of prosperity. Amos mentions mansions and people who own "vacation" homes as if that was not rare. It is a time of luxury and recreation, of "beds of ivory" and eating well and musical innovations (Amos 6:4-5).

Israel and Judah both have stable governments because of kings with long reigns (Israel's Jeroboam II for 40 years, Judah's Uzziah for 51 years). The Assyrian empire is beset with internal issues, so it cannot threaten them. Israel and Judah are surrounded by pagan neighbors, but because of their history as the people of God, they see themselves as superior to their neighbors, and assume their recent prosperity is a sign of God's blessing and the beginning of renewed power and prestige as in the time of David and Solomon. Be aware of a prevailing satiric tone used by Amos in the face of Israel's self-satisfied delusions of security.

<u>Opening Idea:</u> Imagine that a man you had never heard of before, a sheep rancher from Canada, was telling whoever would listen that America was going to be destroyed by another nation within 20-30 years, and this would be an act of God's judgment against America's sinfulness. How would you probably view such a message from such a messenger? What reasons would you have for believing him or ignoring him?

- We would probably wonder why we should listen to a man with no verified authority and from a common background. It could be taken as the jealous rantings of a person who has something against our country.
- The reasons we might believe him is that great nations have fallen many times in history, and we could point to examples of social injustice and endemic sin in America.
- We might not believe him because our prosperity and military strength make such predictions seem far-fetched. We also are a religious country, with "In God We Trust" on our coins, and a large percentage of our citizens in churches. We could point to all the times America has fought against tyranny and poured money into other countries devastated by natural disasters. We would see many reasons, compared to other countries in the world, that God would "prefer" us and want to bless us, not destroy us.
- Many of the same rationales and conditions could be found in Israel when Amos came from its neighbor Judah to prophecy Israel's imminent downfall.

Bad Neighbors

When Amos arrives in Israel, he begins his message by preaching against Israel's neighbors. He runs through a list of neighboring nations and cites specific grievances that God has against each, along with the promise of God's punishment or judgment against them.

The idiom "for three transgressions . . . and for four" probably expresses the use of the number 7 as symbolic of totality or completeness, meaning the wickedness of these nations was complete and they were "ripe" for judgment.

Here is a sample of what those prophecies sounded like:

Amos 1:13-2:2 (NIV)

13 This is what the Lord says:
"For three sins of Ammon, even for four, I will not relent.
Because he ripped open the pregnant women of Gilead
in order to extend his borders,
14 I will set fire to the walls of Rabbah that will consume her fortresses
amid war cries on the day of battle, amid violent winds on a stormy day.
15 Her king will go into exile, he and his officials together," says the Lord.
2 This is what the Lord says: "For three sins of Moab, even for four, I will not relent.
Because he burned to ashes the bones of Edom's king,
2 I will send fire on Moab that will consume the fortresses of Kerioth.
Moab will go down in great tumult amid war cries and the blast of the trumpet.

<u>Group Discussion:</u> It's noteworthy that all of the prophecies against Israel's pagan neighbor – Philistia, Tyre, Edom, and Ammon – are for brutalities committed against Israel. However, the prophecy against Moab is based on what Moab did to Edom, not to Israel. Why is that significant?

- This shows that God is not simply motivated by vengeance against His people's enemies, but that He cares about justice for all people.

If we outline this sermon, we see a very deliberate strategy on the part of Amos.

1. He begins (1:3 – 2:3) by preaching against Israel's foreign enemies on all sides for slave trafficking, warring against God's people, and wanton brutality. These were crimes against humanity.
2. Then he preaches against Judah, Israel's "brother nation," because they rejected God's Law and chose to worship other gods (2:4-5).
3. Finally, he preaches against Israel itself in 2:6-13:

Amos 2:6-13 (NIV)

6 This is what the Lord says: "For three sins of Israel, even for four, I will not turn back my wrath. They sell the righteous for silver, and the needy for a pair of sandals. 7 They trample on the heads of the poor as upon the dust of the ground and deny justice to the oppressed. Father and son use the same girl and so profane my holy name. 8 They lie down beside every altar on garments taken in pledge. In the house of their god they drink wine taken as fines. 9 "I destroyed the Amorite before them, though he was tall as the cedars and strong as the oaks. I destroyed his fruit above and his roots below. 10 "I brought you up out of Egypt, and I led you forty years in the desert to give you the land of the Amorites. 11 I also raised up prophets from among your sons and Nazirites from among your young men. Is this not true, people of Israel?" declares the Lord. 12 "But you made the Nazirites drink wine and commanded the prophets not to prophesy. 13 Now then, I will crush you as a cart crushes when loaded with grain.

Verse 8 "same girl" – probably refers to Baal worship where men would have sex with temple prostitutes to stimulate Baal (the god of fertility) to make their fields or herds fertile.

Verse 8 "garments taken in pledge" – because clothing was so expensive, Mosaic Law required that if a coat was given as collateral for a loan, it had to be returned to the owner each night so that he could sleep in it. Cloaks often doubled as blankets for many people.

Verse 9 "wine taken as fines" – probably refers to rewards given in lawsuits. This suggests a litigation-crazed society that constantly sued each other.

<u>Group Discussion:</u> Why would Amos structure his message in this way? How is this intended to affect his Israelite audience?

- He started by preaching against Israel's enemies. This would have made him popular with the Israelites. Then he preaches against Judah, their "cousins." This would have been popular too, although there is a difference in that the pagan nations were condemned for crimes against humanity, while Judah was condemned for crimes against God.
- But then Amos uses the same formula against Israel, and it would have effectively been shocking to them. They suddenly see themselves as being no different than the despicable nations around them. They are not God's special people; in fact they are worse than all the rest because they violated both common human decency and God's commands. Of all the people, they should have known better.

Amos 3:2 (NIV)

2 "You only have I chosen of all the families of the earth; therefore I will punish you for all your sins."

<u>Group Discussion:</u> God's special relationship with Israel and Judah makes their transgressions all the worse. The implication is because of what God has done for them, and how they knew God, they should have known better. Do you think God still holds some nations to a higher standard because of how He has blessed them or revealed Himself to them?

- See Luke 12:47-48.

Amos the activist

The assumption that crimes (social offenses) are sins (offenses against God) lies at the heart of Amos's sociology. Amos is a champion of social justice. Except for Judah, all the other nations that Amos preached against in chapters 1 and 2 had angered God because of social injustice . He notes that the Lord is concerned with how they treat others, be it through business dealings, legal proceedings, or just selfish callousness:

Amos 2:7-8 (NIV)
7 *They trample on the heads of the poor as on the dust of the ground and deny justice to the oppressed. Father and son use the same girl and so profane my holy name.*
8 *They lie down beside every altar on garments taken in pledge.*
In the house of their god they drink wine taken as fines.

Amos 4:1 (NIV)
Hear this word, you cows of Bashan on Mount Samaria, you women who oppress the poor and crush the needy and say to your husbands, "Bring us some drinks!"

Amos 8:4–5 (NIV)
Hear this, you who trample the needy and do away with the poor of the land, 5 *saying, "When will the New Moon be over that we may sell grain, and the Sabbath be ended that we may market wheat?"— skimping the measure, boosting the price and cheating with dishonest scales,*

Amos 5:12-15 (NIV)
12 *For I know how many are your offenses and how great your sins.*
You oppress the righteous and take bribes and you deprive the poor of justice in the courts.
13 *Therefore the prudent man keeps quiet in such times, for the times are evil.*
14 *Seek good, not evil, that you may live.*
Then the Lord God Almighty will be with you, just as you say he is.
15 *Hate evil, love good; maintain justice in the courts.*
Perhaps the Lord God Almighty will have mercy on the remnant of Joseph.

Amos 5:21-24 (NIV)
21 *"I hate, I despise your religious feasts; I cannot stand your assemblies.*
22 *Even though you bring me burnt offerings and grain offerings, I will not accept them. Though you bring choice fellowship offerings, I will have no regard for them.*
23 *Away with the noise of your songs! I will not listen to the music of your harps.*
24 *But let justice roll on like a river, righteousness like a never-failing stream!*

<u>Group Discussion:</u> What are God's priorities in these passages? How does Amos link social justice to following God?

- God values justice, righteousness, and goodness
- If the people don't share God's values, their religious activities are not just meaningless, they are offensive. If they don't work for what is good socially, what they do for the good God religiously is hypocritical and actually angers Him even more.
- In Amos 4:4-5, the prophet gives a sarcastic "blessing" that equates their religious rituals to rebellion. Their religion is a mockery based on their unethical, selfish lifestyles.

<u>Group Discussion:</u> To what extent, if any, should we apply Amos' link between social justice and religion to modern Christianity? Should social justice and activism be a priority for Christians today?

In **Amos 4:6-12**, Amos lists several recent natural disasters that were meant to be warnings to Israel. Amos shows that they were fulfillments of the warning given by Moses in **Deuteronomy 28:15-68** of what would happen *"if you are not careful to obey all the words of this Law, which are written in this scroll, by fearing this glorious and awesome name – Yahweh, your God . . ."* (Deut 28:56 HCSB).

So Amos sarcastically "introduces" the people to Yahweh again, whom they have ignored for so long:

Amos 4:12-13 (HCSB)
12 *Therefore, Israel, that is what I will do to you, and since I will do that to you,*
Israel, prepare to meet your God!
13 *He is here: the One who forms the mountains, creates the wind, and reveals His thoughts to man, the One who makes the dawn out of darkness and strides on the heights of the earth. Yahweh, the God of Hosts, is His name.*

Amos makes a second "introduction" to Yahweh in Amos 5:8

Amos 5:8 (NIV)
8 *He who made the Pleiades and Orion, who turns midnight into dawn*
and darkens day into night, who calls for the waters of the sea
and pours them out over the face of the land— the Lord is his name.

And again in Amos 9:5-6:

Amos 9:5-6 (NIV)
5 *The Lord, the Lord Almighty—he touches the earth and it melts,*
and all who live in it mourn; the whole land rises like the Nile,
then sinks like the river of Egypt;
6 *he builds his lofty palace in the heavens and sets its foundation on the earth;*
he calls for the waters of the sea and pours them out over the face of the land—
the Lord is his name

<u>Group Discussion:</u> What are these introductions to God and His nature intended to do or to teach?

- They describe God's power. He is not a God to be trifled with.
- They also remind the Israelites that such a God cannot be escaped or avoided. They have ignored all the warning signs of God's displeasure in their recent history – drought, famine, pestilence, crop failure – and instead comforted themselves with their current wealth and military strength. That is a delusion. God is preparing their punishment despite their current sense of blessedness, and they will soon "meet their God" in every sense of that phrase.

Amos continues to give warnings and examples of why the Israelites current sense of invulnerability or righteousness is delusional.

Amos 5:27 (NIV)
27 *Therefore I will send you into exile beyond Damascus,"*
says the Lord, whose name is God Almighty.

This is exactly what will happen when Assyria comes from that direction and carries them off to exile, even though in the time of Amos, Assyria was not seen as a threat.

As further warning, Amos lists several cities in Amos 6:2 that were great in their time, but in the time of Amos are conquered or destroyed:

- Calneh – a Syrian city destroyed by Assyria in the mid-ninth century;
- Hamath – a Syrian city conquered by Jeroboam II, king of Israel during the time of Amos;
- Gath – a Philistine city destroyed by king Ussiah of Judah, another contemporary of Amos.

The Israelites live in luxury and leisure and assume no violence will befall them despite evidence to the contrary with these conquered cities around them proving such things happen all the time!

<u>Group Discussion:</u> Are we ever guilty of the same sort of thinking? On what have you seen people base their sense of rightness, blessedness or security?

Changing God's mind

Amos 7-9 describes a series of five visions God gave to his prophet. They could be illustrated this way (VanGemeren 133):

Locusts (7:1-3)	Fire (7:4-6)	Plumbline (7:7-9)	Fruit Basket (8:1-2)	Temple (8:3)
Suspension of judgment		Judgment is inevitable		Consequences of judgment

One of the most striking aspects of these visions is the apparent power of Amos' intercessory prayers to influence God's actions. Notice that in the first two visions, God relents after Amos begs for mercy on Israel, but in the next two visions God says that judgment is inevitable. It will and must come.

Amos 7:1-9 (NIV)

This is what the Sovereign Lord showed me: He was preparing swarms of locusts after the king's share had been harvested and
just as the second crop was coming up. 2 When they had stripped the land clean, I cried out, "Sovereign Lord, forgive! How can
Jacob survive? He is so small!"
3 So the Lord relented.
"This will not happen," the Lord said.
4 This is what the Sovereign Lord showed me: The Sovereign Lord was calling for judgment by fire; it dried up the great deep
and devoured the land. 5 Then I cried out, "Sovereign Lord, I beg you, stop! How can Jacob survive? He is so small!"
6 So the Lord relented.
"This will not happen either," the Sovereign Lord said.
7 This is what he showed me: The Lord was standing by a wall that had been built true to plumb, with a plumb line in his
hand. 8 And the Lord asked me, "What do you see, Amos?"
"A plumb line," I replied.
Then the Lord said, "Look, I am setting a plumb line among my people Israel; I will spare them no longer.
9 "The high places of Isaac will be destroyed
and the sanctuaries of Israel will be ruined;
with my sword I will rise against the house of Jeroboam."

Amos 8:1-3 (NIV)
This is what the Sovereign Lord showed me: a basket of ripe fruit. 2 *"What do you see, Amos?" he asked.*
"A basket of ripe fruit," I answered.
Then the Lord said to me, "The time is ripe for my people Israel; I will spare them no longer.
3 *"In that day," declares the Sovereign Lord, "the songs in the temple will turn to wailing. Many, many bodies—flung everywhere! Silence!"*

<u>Group Discussion:</u> What applications, if any, can we make from this about the power of prayer – what it can and cannot do? (See also James 5:13-18)

- God may withhold physical pain, illness, punishment or consequences because of our intercessory prayers, but those are temporary fixes for earthly problems. Our prayers cannot repeal the ultimate judgment for unrepentant people. We cannot change the ultimate spiritual destination of people who refuse to acknowledge God. Our prayers do not trump God's ultimate justice.
- A helpful illustration is a stream of water representing the will of God. Much like a stream can be diverted into different channels, God may respond to our prayers by diverting or changing course, at least temporarily. But like a stream that may take numerous curves and various channels, it will always run downhill, God's will can take many different paths, but His will is always ultimately done.

Amos 9:11 starts a new section with a much different tone, not of punishment, but of restoration. Notice how that restoration is begun:

Amos 9:11-12 (NIV)
11 *"In that day "I will restore David's fallen shelter—I will repair its broken walls*
and restore its ruins— and will rebuild it as it used to be,
12 *so that they may possess the remnant of Edom and all the nations that bear my name,"*
declares the Lord, who will do these things.

<u>Group Discussion:</u> Why would David be significant to the northern kingdom of Israel and its restoration?

- The divided kingdom began when Israel rejected David's line and broke off as a separate kingdom, which then led to idol worship in Bethel as an alternative to the Temple in Jerusalem, the City of David. Also, Jesus will come from the line of David and will restore "all nations."

Amos 9:13-15 (NIV)
13 *"The days are coming," declares the Lord,*
"when the reaper will be overtaken by the plowman and the planter by the one treading grapes. New wine will drip from the mountains and flow from all the hills,
14 *and I will bring my people Israel back from exile. "They will rebuild the ruined cities and live in them. They will plant vineyards and drink their wine; they will make gardens and eat their fruit.*
15 *I will plant Israel in their own land, never again to be uprooted from the land I have given them," says the Lord God.*

<u>Group Discussion:</u> Is this talking about the physical restoration of the northern kingdom of Israel, or is this something more spiritual in nature? Why?

- The abundance described in this section is physically impossible in nature.
- The permanence of the security promised here seems to be eternal.

<u>Group Discussion:</u> Do you think God still judges entire nations, and coordinates the toppling of governments or uses wars as an act of judgment as we see in Amos?

5
OBADIAH
Pride and Prejudice

Brother against brother

While Obadiah is prophesying about the nation of Edom, he is prophesying to the Israelites. At this point, God's people are in exile, waiting for God to deliver on His promises of returning them to their country and bringing His judgment against the nations that persecuted them.

The people of Edom had a long history with the Israelites. In a way, they were "brothers" because of their common ancestry that dated all the way back to the twin sons of Isaac – Jacob and Esau. Jacob was the father of the nation of Israel; Esau became the father of the nation of Edom.

Genesis 25:21-28 (NIV)
21 Isaac prayed to the Lord on behalf of his wife, because she was barren. The Lord answered his prayer, and his wife Rebekah became pregnant. 22 The babies jostled each other within her, and she said, "Why is this happening to me?" So she went to inquire of the Lord.
23 The Lord said to her,
"Two nations are in your womb,
and two peoples from within you will be separated;
one people will be stronger than the other,
and the older will serve the younger."
24 When the time came for her to give birth, there were twin boys in her womb. 25 The first to come out was red, and his whole body was like a hairy garment; so they named him Esau. 26 After this, his brother came out, with his hand grasping Esau's heel; so he was named Jacob. Isaac was sixty years old when Rebekah gave birth to them.
27 The boys grew up, and Esau became a skillful hunter, a man of the open country, while Jacob was a quiet man, staying among the tents. 28 Isaac, who had a taste for wild game, loved Esau, but Rebekah loved Jacob.

From the beginning, these two brothers were competing. Esau was compulsive, bellicose, and irresponsible. Jacob was calculating and deceptive, but also the one God chose to carry on the covenant that would make Israel His chosen people.

Esau claimed the hill country called Seir. Ironically, the outdoorsman named Edom or "red" settled in a wild, mountainous country marked by reddish rock formations southeast of the Dead Sea. From these high places, surrounded by formidable terrain like a natural fortress, the Edomites felt very secure. The King's Highway, the easternmost road connecting Egypt with Aram (Syria) and Mesopotamia, ran north-south through the middle of this territory; other major routes connected Edom with trade throughout the Fertile Crescent and constituted its primary source of revenue. Copper mines in the Seir mountain range also contributed to Edom's wealth (Myers, *Eerdmans*).

Their fierce independence and animosity towards Israel could be traced all the way back to the "blessing" Esau received from his father Isaac. Since Jacob (Israel) had basically stolen the blessing normally given to the oldest son, this was all his father could say for Esau:

Genesis 27:34-40 (NIV)
34 When Esau heard his father's words, he burst out with a loud and bitter cry and said to his father, "Bless me—me too, my father!"
35 But he said, "Your brother came deceitfully and took your blessing."
36 Esau said, "Isn't he rightly named Jacob? He has deceived me these two times: He took my birthright, and now he's taken my blessing!" Then he asked, "Haven't you reserved any blessing for me?"
37 Isaac answered Esau, "I have made him lord over you and have made all his relatives his servants, and I have sustained him with grain and new wine. So what can I possibly do for you, my son?"
38 Esau said to his father, "Do you have only one blessing, my father? Bless me too, my father!" Then Esau wept aloud.
39 His father Isaac answered him,
"Your dwelling will be away from the earth's richness, away from the dew of heaven above.
40 You will live by the sword and you will serve your brother. But when you grow restless, you will throw his yoke from off your neck."

That blessing proved prophetic. The relationship between the descendants of Esau and Jacob was always distrustful. Centuries later, when the Israelites (of Jacob) were being led by Moses towards the Promised Land, they encountered again the Edomites (of Esau).

Numbers 20:14-21 (NIV)
14 Moses sent messengers from Kadesh to the king of Edom, saying:
"This is what your brother Israel says: You know about all the hardships that have come on us. 15 Our ancestors went down
into Egypt, and we lived there many years. The Egyptians mistreated us and our ancestors, 16 but when we cried out to
the Lord, he heard our cry and sent an angel and brought us out of Egypt.
"Now we are here at Kadesh, a town on the edge of your territory. 17 Please let us pass through your country. We will not go through any field or vineyard, or drink water from any well. We will travel along the King's Highway and not turn to the right or to the left until we have passed through your territory."
18 But Edom answered:
"You may not pass through here; if you try, we will march out and attack you with the sword."
19 The Israelites replied:
"We will go along the main road, and if we or our livestock drink any of your water, we will pay for it. We only want to pass through on foot—nothing else."
20 Again they answered:
"You may not pass through."
Then Edom came out against them with a large and powerful army. 21 Since Edom refused to let them go through their
territory, Israel turned away from them.

Sometimes the Edomites were treated as brothers (Deut. 23:7). In comparison, the Moabites and Amorites were explicitly forbidden to enter the assembly of the Lord, not even to the tenth generation, but Edomites were permitted to enter after the third generation (Deut 23:7-8).

But the common ancestry did not prevent frequent wars between these two peoples. The Edomites fought against David (2 Sam 8:13-14) and Solomon (1 Kings 11:14-25), and against the Judean kings Jehoshaphat (2 Chron. 20), and his son Jehoram (2 Kings 8:20-22).

Just like Esau was the jealous older brother who saw his birthright and blessing taken by the younger Jacob, so did Edom watch jealously from the hills as Israel prospered nearby. Amos 1:11 described Edom's attitude like this: "*his anger raged continually and his fury flamed unchecked.*"

All that jealousy and pride ignited into dark cruelty when Judah was crushed by an invasion of Babylonians in 605-586 BC, and the Edomites saw a chance to not only gloat over the fall of their cousins, but do much worse.

Pride goes before the fall

Obadiah 1-4 (NIV)
The vision of Obadiah. This is what the Sovereign Lord says about Edom—
We have heard a message from the Lord: An envoy was sent to the nations to say,
"Rise, and let us go against her for battle"—
2 *"See, I will make you small among the nations; you will be utterly despised.*
3 *The pride of your heart has deceived you, you who live in the clefts of the rocks*
and make your home on the heights, you who say to yourself, 'Who can bring me down to the ground?'
4 *Though you soar like the eagle and make your nest among the stars, from there I will bring you down," declares the Lord.*

It is assumed this prophecy happened after the fall of Judah, but the Edomites were apparently not threatened by the invasion of their neighbor. Until now. The prophet is giving Edom advanced warning of an intrigue among other nations to attack them. He does not warn them so they can save themselves. They won't be able to save themselves. There will be no escape from this coming storm because this is orchestrated by the hand of the inescapable God.

Obadiah 5-9 (NIV)
5 *"If thieves came to you,*
if robbers in the night—
Oh, what a disaster awaits you—
would they not steal only as much as they wanted?
If grape pickers came to you,
would they not leave a few grapes?
6 *But how Esau will be ransacked,*
his hidden treasures pillaged!
7 *All your allies will force you to the border;*
your friends will deceive and overpower you;
those who eat your bread will set a trap for you,
but you will not detect it.
8 *"In that day," declares the Lord,*
"will I not destroy the wise men of Edom,
men of understanding in the mountains of Esau?
9 *Your warriors, O Teman, will be terrified,*
and everyone in Esau's mountains will be cut down in the slaughter.

Jeremiah, another prophet who lived at the same time, delivered a very similar prophecy against Edom. He also uses the analogy of thieves and grape pickers, but adds a little more to the description of Edom's utter desolation:

Jeremiah 49:10-11 (NIV)
10 But I will strip Esau bare; I will uncover his hiding places, so that he cannot conceal himself.
His armed men are destroyed, also his allies and neighbors, so there is no one to say,
11 'Leave your fatherless children; I will keep them alive. Your widows too can depend on me.'"

<u>Group Discussion:</u> Why do Obadiah and Jeremiah stress the completeness of the overthrow of Edom? Why use the comparison with thieves and grape pickers?

- If the coming destruction is just the work of thieves, or just of human ambitions, then they would not be so completely destroyed. But so that they will know it is the work of the inescapable God, their punishment will come with the completeness of Divine judgment.
- This is reminiscent of the Flood, another time when Divine Judgment was unquestionably from God because the destruction was so complete.

What does God have against us?

Jeremiah does not explain the reason for Edom's punishment, but Obadiah does: It is because of how Edom reacts when Judah is laid low by foreign invaders.

Obadiah 10-14 (NIV)
10 Because of the violence against your brother Jacob, you will be covered with shame; you will be destroyed forever.
11 On the day you stood aloof while strangers carried off his wealth and foreigners entered his gates and cast lots for Jerusalem, you were like one of them.
12 You should not look down on your brother in the day of his misfortune, nor rejoice over the people of Judah in the day of their destruction, nor boast so much in the day of their trouble.
13 You should not march through the gates of my people in the day of their disaster, nor look down on them in their calamity in the day of their disaster, nor seize their wealth in the day of their disaster.
14 You should not wait at the crossroads to cut down their fugitives, nor hand over their survivors in the day of their trouble.

Most scholars believe these specific complaints against Edom happened after Jerusalem was attacked and the Judeans carried into exile by Babylon in 586 B.C. This was the horrible time mentioned by many prophets like Jeremiah. It was during this time that Daniel and others were carried off.

<u>Group Discussion:</u> If the Babylonian exile was God's justice, if it was Judah getting what it deserved and what it had been warned about for generations, then why is God angry at Edom for applauding the discipline of Judah? What are the actions that Obadiah specifically mentions?

- Standing aloof while foreigners carried off Jerusalem made the Edomites accomplices (v. 11).
- Rejoicing and boasting over the misfortune of others (v. 12).
- Taking advantage of Judah's calamity for personal gain (v. 13).
- Oppressing people who are already oppressed or defeated (v. 14).
- Notice the progression of Edom's actions. The first stage was passively observing enemies looting. From passive observation, Edom progressed to 'gloating' or rejoicing over Judah's problems, entering into the very gates (La. 4:12–13) to see more closely, and then even looting their abandoned possessions. Finally, they stooped to attacking the refugees from Judah (2 Ki. 25:4–5), handing the already hard-pressed survivors over to their oppressors (Carson).

The Edomites cheered and gloated while the Judeans received the punishment that God had promised, and that they deserved because of their sinful ways. Yet God chastised Edom for acting this way.

<u>Group Discussion:</u> Do you ever see Christians gloating or cheering over other's punishment or misfortune?

- How have some Christians reacted to the AIDS epidemic among the homosexual community, or after a public flameout of a celebrity?

<u>Group Discussion:</u> So what is the proper Christian reaction when other people seem to be reaping what they have sown?

- Proverbs 24:16-18 (NIV) 16 for though a righteous man falls seven times, he rises again, but the wicked are brought down by calamity. 17 Do not gloat when your enemy falls; when he stumbles, do not let your heart rejoice, 18 or the Lord will see and disapprove and turn his wrath away from him.
- Jude 22-23 (NIV) 22 Be merciful to those who doubt; 23 snatch others from the fire and save them; to others show mercy, mixed with fear—hating even the clothing stained by corrupted flesh.
- 1 Corinthians 13:4-6 (NIV) 4 Love is patient, love is kind. It does not envy, it does not boast, it is not proud. 5 It is not rude, it is not self-seeking, it is not easily angered, it keeps no record of wrongs. 6 Love does not delight in evil but rejoices with the truth.

<u>Group Discussion:</u> Why is this the response God wants from us when we see others who might be getting rightfully disciplined by Him?

- As parents, when we discipline one child, we resent when the other children try to jump in. In Edom's case, God was saying that discipline should come from the Father, not the brother.
- No one likes a bad winner. Gloating is never attractive. Empathy, on the other hand, may bring these people closer to us where we can minister to them.

God's discipline is less severe than God's judgment. As parents, we spank or scold when our children leave the yard because getting run over in the street would be much worse. God's discipline in our earthly lives is a warning that turns us from what waits eternally if we don't repent and reform. God overthrew Jerusalem so that at a future time His humbled people would return to Him. Edom reveled in Judah's discipline, not recognizing that there was a message in it for them as well. Indeed, the message is for all nations.

Obadiah 15-16 (NIV)

15 *"The day of the Lord is near for all nations.*
As you have done, it will be done to you; your deeds will return upon your own head.
16 *Just as you drank on my holy hill, so all the nations will drink continually;*
they will drink and drink and be as if they had never been.

<u>Group Discussion:</u> This idea of nations drinking themselves into oblivion is an odd allegory. What are they drinking? What is Obadiah saying here?

- They are "drinking" or receiving God's wrath.
- Compare this to another drinking allegory in **Jeremiah 25:15-16, 27-29 (NIV):** *15 This is what the Lord, the God of Israel, said to me: "Take from my hand this cup filled with the wine of my wrath and make all the nations to whom I send you drink it. 16 When they drink it, they will stagger and go mad because of the sword I will send among them." . . . 27 "Then tell them, 'This is what the Lord Almighty, the God of Israel, says: Drink, get drunk and vomit, and fall to rise no more because of the sword I will send among you.' 28 But if they refuse to take the cup from your hand and drink, tell them, 'This is what the Lord Almighty says: You must drink it! 29 See, I am beginning to bring disaster on the city that bears my Name, and will you indeed go unpunished? You will not go unpunished, for I am calling down a sword upon all who live on the earth, declares the Lord Almighty.'*
- Instead of rejoicing at Israel's downfall through drunken revelry in Jerusalem, God's holy hill, they will now drink totally the cup of God's wrath, and this is not a cup they can refuse.

Obadiah 17-18 (NIV)
[17] But on Mount Zion will be deliverance; it will be holy, and the house of Jacob will possess its inheritance.
[18] The house of Jacob will be a fire and the house of Joseph a flame; the house of Esau will be stubble, and they will set it on fire and consume it. There will be no survivors from the house of Esau." The Lord has spoken.

Edom was conquered by Babylon in 553 BC, 33 years after the fall of Jerusalem. As a people they became known as Idumeans, after Idumea, an area in southern Judah that they settled after the Jews were exiled. Later, during the Persian empire, an Arab people called the Nabateans forced the Edomites out of their native mountains in Edom.

In the second century B.C. Judas Maccabee "fought against the children of Esau in Idumea . . . and he gave them a great overthrow, and abated their courage, and took their spoils" (1 Macc. 5:1-3, 65). Later still, the Jewish leader John Hyrcanus subdued the Edomites further, forcing them to submit to ritual circumcision and conversion to Judaism.

Although a specific time is not given, and the Maccabees may not be the fulfillment of this, Ezekiel did prophesy that Israel would successfully wage war against Edom.

Ezekiel 25:12-14 (NIV)
[12] "This is what the Sovereign Lord says: 'Because Edom took revenge on Judah and became very guilty by doing so, [13] therefore this is what the Sovereign Lord says: I will stretch out my hand against Edom and kill both man and beast. I will lay it waste, and from Teman to Dedan they will fall by the sword. [14] I will take vengeance on Edom by the hand of my people Israel, and they will deal with Edom in accordance with my anger and my wrath; they will know my vengeance, declares the Sovereign Lord.'"

Herod the Great traced his ancestry back to a converted Idumean. In *The Jewish War* Josephus described how Edomites sided with the Zealots against the Jewish "establishment" and massacred more than 20,000 of Jerusalem's inhabitants. With the fall of Jerusalem in A.D. 70, the Edomites dropped out of recorded history (VanGemeren 145-146).

Jeremiah 49:17-18 (NIV)
[17] "Edom will become an object of horror; all who pass by will be appalled and will scoff because of all its wounds.
[18] As Sodom and Gomorrah were overthrown, along with their neighboring towns," says the Lord, "so no one will live there; no people will dwell in it.

Today, there are no Edomites. They have disappeared as a people, just as Malachi predicted:

Malachi 1:3 (NIV)
[3] . . . but Esau I have hated, and I have turned his hill country into a wasteland and left his inheritance to the desert jackals.

Whose kingdom is this anyway?

The last few verses of Obadiah present some translation problems because it uses some obscure Hebrew words and some place names that are not easily identified. However, the underlying message is still very clear.

Obadiah 19-21 (NIV)
19 People from the Negev will occupy the mountains of Esau,
and people from the foothills will possess the land of the Philistines.
They will occupy the fields of Ephraim and Samaria, and Benjamin will possess Gilead.
20 This company of Israelite exiles who are in Canaan will possess the land as far as Zarephath;
the exiles from Jerusalem who are in Sepharad will possess the towns of the Negev.
21 Deliverers will go up on Mount Zion to govern the mountains of Esau. And the kingdom will be the Lord's.

If you look at a map while reading this passage, you will see that God is essentially saying that His people will at some point again possess all of their inheritance. This is the message of hope Obadiah offered the exiled Israelites, and indeed this all happened. The Israelites did return from exile to their land, and the Philistines and Edomites did completely disappear. This is all ancient history, so is there any useful application from the second half of Obadiah for us today?

The last sentence of Obadiah, "the kingdom will be the Lord's," transcends time. It is a prophetic statement that reaches every nation in every age. It is echoed many times in the Bible:

- Daniel 2:44 (NIV) 44 "In the time of those kings, the God of heaven will set up a kingdom that will never be destroyed, nor will it be left to another people. It will crush all those kingdoms and bring them to an end, but it will itself endure forever.
- Revelation 11:15 (NIV) 15 The seventh angel sounded his trumpet, and there were loud voices in heaven, which said: "The kingdom of the world has become the kingdom of our Lord and of his Christ, and he will reign for ever and ever."
- Authority over all the kingdoms of this world is Jesus' destiny. He is King of kings (1 Tim. 6:15).

<u>Group Discussion:</u> If this is the final outcome of all nations, including ours, how should this influence our relationship with our nation, our government?

- This does not discourage patriotism or service in government and the military, but our first allegiance is not to our country, but to our God. We are first citizens of God's kingdom before we are citizens of any earthly kingdom. Therefore, our highest priority is the expansion of God's kingdom, not the preservation of our nation.
- Our hope is in God, not our government. Our provider is God, not our government. It is in God that we trust. That does give us some perspective on the true importance of events like elections. We know that God is still in control.

6
JONAH
Letting God out of our box

Jonah as a book is problematic for many Bible readers. In one sense, it is a refreshing break from many of the minor prophets because it tells an engaging story in simple, linear form. Except for one segment of poetry/prayer in chapter 2, this is straight narrative. The problem with Jonah is not in understanding it, but believing it. Most objections to the validity of Jonah as historical truth are objections to the believability of things like Jonah surviving for three days inside a big fish; or of one man's ability to preach in a way that convinces an entire large city, an enemy city, to stop in mass repentance in less than two days. Perhaps the best evidence for deciding how to interpret Jonah is what Jesus said about him.

Matthew 12:38-41 (NIV)
38 Then some of the Pharisees and teachers of the law said to him, "Teacher, we want to see a miraculous sign from you."
39 He answered, "A wicked and adulterous generation asks for a miraculous sign! But none will be given it except the sign of the prophet Jonah. 40 For as Jonah was three days and three nights in the belly of a huge fish, so the Son of Man will be three days and three nights in the heart of the earth. 41 The men of Nineveh will stand up at the judgment with this generation and condemn it; for they repented at the preaching of Jonah, and now one greater than Jonah is here.

<u>Group Discussion:</u> Based on what Jesus says about Jonah and his story, would you consider everything in the book of Jonah to be historical fact or some sort of fable or parable?

- Jesus compares Jonah's time in the belly of a huge fish to how he will be in the grave for three days. Since Jesus was literally in the grave for that time, it would appear that Jonah was literally in the belly of a fish for three days.
- *Three days and three nights* is a special phrase used in the ancient world with the meaning 'long enough to be definitely dead'. It derives originally from the ancient pagan notion that the soul's trip to the after-world took three days and nights. Jesus' use of the same phrase for the duration of his death before his resurrection (Mt. 12:40) carries a similar force: it is a way of saying that he would really die, not that he would be literally dead for exactly seventy-two hours (Carson, *New Bible Commentary*).
- Also, Jesus speaks about the men of Nineveh at judgment. We know from all his teachings that Jesus viewed the Judgment Day as something very real. He also views what happened in Nineveh through the preaching of Jonah as something that was very real. It would make no sense for Jesus to predict that characters from a fictional story will be involved in the very serious and real events of Judgment.

Jonah also exists as a real person elsewhere in the Old Testament. He was a nationally-known prophet associated with a time when Israel recovered lost territory and restored their traditional borders. Israel was feeling ascendant and powerfully secure under Jeroboam II:

2 Kings 14:23-25 (NIV)
23 In the fifteenth year of Amaziah son of Joash king of Judah, Jeroboam son of Jehoash king of Israel became king in Samaria, and he reigned forty-one years. 24 He did evil in the eyes of the Lord and did not turn away from any of the sins of Jeroboam son of Nebat, which he had caused Israel to commit. 25 He was the one who restored the boundaries of Israel from Lebo Hamath to the Sea of the Arabah, in accordance with the word of the Lord, the God of Israel, spoken through his servant Jonah son of Amittai, the prophet from Gath Hepher.

After sharing a message of victory for the Israelites, a message that no doubt would have made him popular, Jonah receives another assignment from God:

Jonah 1:1-3 (NIV)
1 The word of the Lord came to Jonah son of Amittai: 2 "Go to the great city of Nineveh and preach against it, because its wickedness has come up before me."
3 But Jonah ran away from the Lord and headed for Tarshish. He went down to Joppa, where he found a ship bound for that port. After paying the fare, he went aboard and sailed for Tarshish to flee from the Lord .

Nineveh was established by Nimrod, a mighty warrior and hunter, and the ancestor of both Babylon and Assyria (Genesis 10:8-12). Nimrod came from the line of Ham, the son cursed by Noah for shaming his father (Genesis 9:22-25). The cursed Ham was also the ancestor of other traditional enemies of Israel like Egypt and the Canaanites. So the enmity between Israel and Assyria dates all the way back to Noah.

The city of Nineveh was located on the east side of the Tigris River about 550 miles northeast of Samaria. That distance required a journey of more than a month, if Jonah traveled the normal distance of 15-20 miles a day. It was in modern-day Iraq opposite the modern town of Mosul. When Jonah tries to run away from God, he literally goes in the opposite direction of where he was called. Instead of going east towards Nineveh, he heads directly west towards Tarshish, modern day Spain, which was the edge of the known world at that time.

Nineveh was the capital of the Assyrian empire, one of the cruelest, vilest, most powerful, and most idolatrous empires in the world and a long-time enemy of Israel. As an example, the Assyrian king Ashurbanipal (669-626) described his treatment of a captured leader in these words: "I pierced his chin with my hand dagger. Through his jaw . . . I passed a rope, put a dog chain upon him and made him occupy . . . a kennel". In his campaign against Egypt, Ashurbanipal also boasted that his officials hung Egyptian corpses"on stakes [and] stripped off their skins and covered the city wall(s) with them". No wonder the Biblical prophet Nahum called Nineveh "the city of blood" (3:1), a city noted for its "cruelty"! (3:19) Amos and Hosea, both contemporaries of Jonah, prophesied that Assyria would oppress and destroy Israel (Walvoord, *Bible Knowledge Commentary).*

<u>Group Discussion:</u> So with that historical background, what are some possible explanations for Jonah's behavior? Why would he not want to go and preach to Nineveh?

- Fear of the bloodthirsty Assyrians.
- Fear that he will be considered a traitor to his own people.
- Fear that he will fail and be humiliated.
- Fear that he will succeed and God will show compassion to this evil people.

The book of Jonah is an amazing little piece of literature held together by the tension between contrasts. Instead of leading towards one satisfying, unifying climax, it ends abruptly with God getting the last word and Jonah remaining a whining ninny. As we read this story, look for contrasts like these: the contrast between what Jonah is commanded to do and what he actually does; the contrast between Jonah's attitude and that of the pagans he meets; the contrast between God's priorities and Jonah's.

Jonah 1:4-17 (NIV)

4 Then the Lord sent a great wind on the sea, and such a violent storm arose that the ship threatened to break up. 5 All the sailors were afraid and each cried out to his own god. And they threw the cargo into the sea to lighten the ship.
But Jonah had gone below deck, where he lay down and fell into a deep sleep. 6 The captain went to him and said, "How can you sleep? Get up and call on your god! Maybe he will take notice of us, and we will not perish."
7 Then the sailors said to each other, "Come, let us cast lots to find out who is responsible for this calamity." They cast lots and the lot fell on Jonah.
8 So they asked him, "Tell us, who is responsible for making all this trouble for us? What do you do? Where do you come from? What is your country? From what people are you?"
9 He answered, "I am a Hebrew and I worship the Lord, the God of heaven, who made the sea and the land."
10 This terrified them and they asked, "What have you done?" (They knew he was running away from the Lord, because he had already told them so.)
11 The sea was getting rougher and rougher. So they asked him, "What should we do to you to make the sea calm down for us?"
12 "Pick me up and throw me into the sea," he replied, "and it will become calm. I know that it is my fault that this great storm has come upon you."
13 Instead, the men did their best to row back to land. But they could not, for the sea grew even wilder than before. 14 Then they cried to the Lord, "O Lord, please do not let us die for taking this man's life. Do not hold us accountable for killing an innocent man, for you, O Lord, have done as you pleased." 15 Then they took Jonah and threw him overboard, and the raging sea grew calm. 16 At this the men greatly feared the Lord, and they offered a sacrifice to the Lord and made vows to him.
17 But the Lord provided a great fish to swallow Jonah, and Jonah was inside the fish three days and three nights.

<u>Group Discussion:</u> Notice the sailors' questions: "What do you do? Where do you come from?" What effect would these questions have on Jonah?

- They forced the bitter prophet to reflect upon his faith. Jonah is being reminded of the things he professes to believe (Briscoe 75). They force him to say out loud the truth he is trying to escape.
- The sailors' willingness to do what is necessary to please God is in sharp contrast to Jonah's callow attempt to duck God.

Jonah 1:17 – 2:10 (NIV)

17 But the Lord provided a great fish to swallow Jonah, and Jonah was inside the fish three days and three nights. From inside the fish Jonah prayed to the Lord his God. 2 He said: "In my distress I called to the Lord , and he answered me. From the depths of the grave I called for help, and you listened to my cry.
3 You hurled me into the deep, into the very heart of the seas, and the currents swirled about me; all your waves and breakers swept over me. 4 I said, 'I have been banished from your sight; yet I will look again toward your holy temple.' 5 The engulfing waters threatened me, the deep surrounded me; seaweed was wrapped around my head. 6 To the roots of the mountains I sank down; the earth beneath barred me in forever. But you brought my life up from the pit, O Lord my God. 7 "When my life was ebbing away, I remembered you, Lord , and my prayer rose to you, to your holy temple. 8 "Those who cling to worthless idols forfeit the grace that could be theirs. 9 But I, with a song of thanksgiving, will sacrifice to you. What I have vowed I will make good. Salvation comes from the Lord ."
10 And the Lord commanded the fish, and it vomited Jonah onto dry land.

Notice the theme throughout the first two chapters of descending or falling:

1. Jonah goes *down* to Joppa (1:3)
2. He goes *down* to the hold of the ship (1:5)
3. He is thrown *down* into the water (1:15)
4. The fish carries him all the way *down* to the "roots of the mountains" on the sea floor (2:6). A person on earth could literally go no lower.
5. Then it is God who brings him "*up* from the pit" (2:6).

Jonah 3:1-5, 10 (NIV)

Then the word of the Lord came to Jonah a second time: 2 "Go to the great city of Nineveh and proclaim to it the message I give you."
3 Jonah obeyed the word of the Lord and went to Nineveh. Now Nineveh was a very important city—a visit required three days. 4 On the first day, Jonah started into the city. He proclaimed: "Forty more days and Nineveh will be overturned." 5 The Ninevites believed God. They declared a fast, and all of them, from the greatest to the least, put on sackcloth.
10 When God saw what they did and how they turned from their evil ways, he had compassion and did not bring upon them the destruction he had threatened.

The size of Nineveh – "a visit required three days" – has been interpreted a few ways. The ESV translates it as "an exceedingly great city, three days journey in breadth." That could mean it would have taken Jonah three days to travel all of its streets preaching. Or it could have encompassed Nineveh and a "metroplex" that included neighboring Rehoboth Ir, Calah and Resen (Genesis 10:11-12), an administrative district 30-56 miles across (ESV Study Bible notes on Jonah 3:3b).

Group Discussion: What was Jonah's message to the Ninevites (read Jonah 3:4)? Obviously, he said more than the one sentence summary we see here, but what could explain his profound success with this simple message? What possible lessons can we learn from that in our own evangelistic efforts today?

- Ancient Assyrian legends credited a being named Oannes with founding the city of Nineveh. Oannes was supposedly part fish and part man. In fact, the cuneiform sign for Nineveh meant "house of fish." The symbolism of a prophet who had been swallowed by a fish may have added to Jonah's credibility with them (Gardner, 366).
- Also, Before Jonah arrived at this fortress-city, two plagues had erupted there (in 765 and 759 b.c.), widespread famine was afflicting parts of the empire, and a total eclipse of the sun occurred on June 15, 763. These were considered signs of divine anger and may help explain why the Ninevites responded so readily to Jonah's message, around 759 (Walvoord, *Bible Knowledge Commentary*).
- The writer probably intentionally reduced Jonah's sermon down to this one-sentence skeleton to emphasize that the power of the message was not in the messenger. It could also show that Jonah was giving a half-hearted effort. It is also noteworthy that verse five says, "The Ninevites believed *God*." The power of this message was that it came from God.
- We can't know what God has been doing in people's hearts that may make them ready to respond to something we say, no matter how simple the message or untalented the messenger.

The Ninevites' repentance was genuine, although temporary. The language of his verse does not imply a permanent repentance, nor a conversion to worshipping Israel's God. The people had acted according to their own religious traditions, on what little they knew, and their actions were graciously accepted by God. About 50 years later, the Assyrians (the nationality of the Ninevites) would destroy Israel. About 90 years after that, Nineveh itself would be destroyed. Now, however, God spared them; just the opposite of what Jonah wanted (Carson, *Bible Knowledge Commentary*).

Jonah 4:1-11 (NIV)

But Jonah was greatly displeased and became angry. 2 He prayed to the Lord , "O Lord , is this not what I said when I was still at home? That is why I was so quick to flee to Tarshish. I knew that you are a gracious and compassionate God, slow to anger and abounding in love, a God who relents from sending calamity. 3 Now, O Lord , take away my life, for it is better for me to die than to live."
4 But the Lord replied, "Have you any right to be angry?"

[5] *Jonah went out and sat down at a place east of the city. There he made himself a shelter, sat in its shade and waited to see what would happen to the city.* [6] *Then the Lord God provided a vine and made it grow up over Jonah to give shade for his head to ease his discomfort, and Jonah was very happy about the vine.* [7] *But at dawn the next day God provided a worm, which chewed the vine so that it withered.* [8] *When the sun rose, God provided a scorching east wind, and the sun blazed on Jonah's head so that he grew faint. He wanted to die, and said, "It would be better for me to die than to live."*
[9] *But God said to Jonah, "Do you have a right to be angry about the vine?"*
"I do," he said. "I am angry enough to die."
[10] *But the Lord said, "You have been concerned about this vine, though you did not tend it or make it grow. It sprang up overnight and died overnight.* [11] *But Nineveh has more than a hundred and twenty thousand people who cannot tell their right hand from their left, and many cattle as well. Should I not be concerned about that great city?"*

<u>Group Discussion:</u> Why would God want Nineveh to repent if they were not His people anyway? How does God answer that in this book or elsewhere in the Old Testament?

There is a paradox that Jonah struggles with. It was indeed the paradox of many prophets. God described it to Jeremiah a few centuries later this way in **Jeremiah 18:7-10 (NIV):** [7] *If at any time I announce that a nation or kingdom is to be uprooted, torn down and destroyed,* [8] *and if that nation I warned repents of its evil, then I will relent and not inflict on it the disaster I had planned.* [9] *And if at another time I announce that a nation or kingdom is to be built up and planted,* [10] *and if it does evil in my sight and does not obey me, then I will reconsider the good I had intended to do for it.*

Jonah's paradox is that the Ninevites respond to his message and repent, and then after the promised 40 days, nothing happens. Day after day goes by, and nothing happens. The Ninevites may begin to wonder if punishment really had been coming at all. The very success of a prophet's message may cause people to doubt the validity of that message. Jonah may have understandably hoped for at least a "little punishment" to strike Nineveh – a few bolts of lightning, a voice from heaven - just to prove to them that they had ducked a much bigger bullet. But the way this story happened, there was no satisfying affirmation for Jonah. He gained nothing personally in the salvation of Nineveh.

<u>Group Discussion:</u> Based on his attitude and actions, what was Jonah's personality like? What were some of the reasons he was unhappy or frustrated?

- Egotistical – Jonah felt spiritually connected or renewed when it was his own life being saved, but he showed no compassion when it was hundreds of thousands of Ninevites who were benefiting.
- Prejudiced – his hate of the Assyrians was greater than his desire to obey God;
- Angry – he became infuriated about things like the vine over which he had no control;
- Misdirected priorities – his priorities were not the same as God's. He did not love the same things God loved. This made him a frustrated servant, and prevented him from even enjoying his successes.
- Life for Jonah is a series of confusing surprises and frustrations. He tries to escape from God and is trapped. He then gives up, expecting to die, and is saved. He obeys when given a second chance, and then is frustrated and embarrassed because his preaching is successful (Mather, 283.).
- Andy Stanley had a great object lesson based on Jonah. He gave each person in his church a potted plant and told them to take it home and let it die, much as the vine shading Jonah died. Jonah became furious and self-pitying over the loss of the vine, but he showed no care for the people in Nineveh who would die without God. The takeaway was a reminder that we care about and get angry about so many things, but do we care as much about people who are dying without knowing God?

<u>Group Discussion:</u> Based on His attitude and actions in the book of Jonah, what is God's personality like? What do we learn about God in this story?

This book doesn't identify its author, but because of its personal nature, it must almost certainly have originated with Jonah himself. Because it casts Jonah in such a poor light at the end, maybe that implies that Jonah shared this because he finally saw his error and the hardness of his heart, and wrote this as a sort of confessional with the clear moral being not to have the same hard heart he did.

It comes down to this: do you believe your Father knows best? Do you really think that God is a just God? Can you see the jerk who annoys you most or has hurt you the worst, can you see him in your heaven? Are you willing to do something for your personal satisfaction that could potentially keep people you don't like out of heaven? If so, your heaven is too small, as is your understanding of God's love.

You cannot forbid the God who loves you from loving someone else too. And if God loves even them, so can you.

7
MICAH
And what does the Lord require of you?

A Voice in a Raging Storm

The book of Micah is actually a collection of many short messages, or oracles, delivered over several years to both Israel and Judah. He prophesied during the reign of three Judean kings: Jotham (750-735 B.C.), Ahaz (735-715 B.C.), and Hezekiah (715-687 B.C.). We don't have dates within the book, so it is hard to say over how long a period the various prophecies within Micah were delivered.

To appreciate Micah, it is essential to understand the times in which he lived and the wave of violent upheaval sweeping through Israel and Judah that served as the backdrop of his messages. In this time period, God's people were a divided kingdom. The northern kingdom of Israel had set up the city of Samaria as their capital, while Jerusalem remained the capital of the southern kingdom of Judah.

Pressured from outside by Assyria while rotting inside from corruption, the northern kingdom of Israel collapsed in 722-721 B.C. After repeated warnings by God through His prophets, and after several encroachments by the Assyrians, the capital city of Samaria was toppled by the Assyrians. Many of the rich and influential people of Israel were carried off to exile, and many of the rest fled to Jerusalem.

The southern kingdom of Judah tended to fare better because of better leadership, but even they were sliding into apostasy and adopting more of the practices of their idolatrous neighbors. They also were losing territory to the Assyrians. It is during this time of fear, of upheaval, of constant war, that Micah prophesies. Micah is a confusing book to just sit down and read. It abruptly skips point-of-view from Micah to God and back again. It also seems scattered because it is a collection of oracles or messages given over several years during the reigns of three very different kings. It helps, however, to read it from the perspective of people always conscious of two threats bearing down on them: (1) internal corruption in their society and religion, and (2) the approaching Assyrian army.

Events during the life of Micah		
Year	**Event**	**Significance**
750	Jotham assumes throne of Judah	He is described in 2 Chron. 27 as doing what was right in the eyes of God, although his people "continued their corrupt practices."
735	Ahaz becomes king of Judah.	A horrible influence on Judah. He encourages idolatry, mixes Jewish and pagan practices, and even sacrifices his own children.
734-732	Tiglath-Pileser II of Assyria conquers large sections of Israel and surrounding nations.	Israel loses much of their territory. Even Judah pays tribute to Assyria. Ahaz empties the temple treasury to pay off Assyria.
721	Sargon II of Assyria topples Israel's capital city of Samaria and carries off 27,000 Israelites into exile.	Ten of the original twelve tribes of God's people are now ruled by Assyria. What so many of them considered impossible has now happened: God's people have been torn from their land, and He did not prevent it. Refugees flood into Jerusalem, which swells to four times its previous population.
715-701	Hezekiah becomes king of Judah.	A righteous reformer, he works to restore the temple and the proper worship of God. Emboldened by the successes God gives him, he refuses to pay tribute to Assyria. After Assyria captures several foothill cities, he relents and sends them a payment, but they come with an army demanding full surrender.
701	The Assyrians come to the very gates of Jerusalem.	After all his reforms and faithfulness, Hezekiah still sees foreign invaders take most of his territory and come to the gates of his capital. He must decide if he should surrender to the Assyrians or trust that God will deliver Jerusalem.

Crime and Punishment

Micah 1:3-5 (NIV)

3 Look! The Lord is coming from his dwelling place; he comes down and treads the high places of the earth.
4 The mountains melt beneath him and the valleys split apart, like wax before the fire, like water rushing down a slope.
5 All this is because of Jacob's transgression, because of the sins of the house of Israel. What is Jacob's transgression? Is it not Samaria? What is Judah's high place? Is it not Jerusalem?

<u>Group Discussion</u>: The book opens with a magnificent vision of the great King entering history. In the light of the twin threats facing Israel and Judah, why is this image of power meaningful?

- It is a reminder that the power of the Assyrian army is no match for God.
- "Treads the high places" predicts how God will stamp out the idol worship in the high places of Israel and Judah. Jerusalem is actually on a mountain, but it is depicted later in this book as just another high place for idol worship, like so many other hills.

Micah 1:6-9 (NIV)

6 "Therefore I will make Samaria a heap of rubble, a place for planting vineyards. I will pour her stones into the valley and lay bare her foundations.
7 All her idols will be broken to pieces; all her temple gifts will be burned with fire; I will destroy all her images. Since she gathered her gifts from the wages of prostitutes, as the wages of prostitutes they will again be used."

[8] *Because of this I will weep and wail; I will go about barefoot and naked. I will howl like a jackal and moan like an owl.*
[9] *For her wound is incurable; it has come to Judah. It has reached the very gate of my people, even to Jerusalem itself.*

Micah predicted the fall of the city of Samaria in the north (722 B.C.), which did happen in his lifetime. Now the same threats – immorality, idolatry, and the Assyrians – have come to his city of Jerusalem.

Micah 2:6-11 (NIV)
[6] *"Do not prophesy," their prophets say. "Do not prophesy about these things; disgrace will not overtake us."*
[7] *Should it be said, O house of Jacob: "Is the Spirit of the Lord angry? Does he do such things?"*
"Do not my words do good to him whose ways are upright?
[8] *Lately my people have risen up like an enemy. You strip off the rich robe from those who pass by without a care, like men returning from battle.*
[9] *You drive the women of my people from their pleasant homes. You take away my blessing from their children forever.*
[10] *Get up, go away! For this is not your resting place, because it is defiled, it is ruined, beyond all remedy.*
[11] *If a liar and deceiver comes and says, 'I will prophesy for you plenty of wine and beer,' he would be just the prophet for this people!*

<u>Group Discussion</u>: The English Standard Version renders Micah 2:11 this way: "If a man should go about and utter wind and lies, saying, 'I will preach to you of wine and strong drink,' he would be the preacher for this people." Is that still something we see today, either among preachers or church-goers?

<u>Group Discussion</u>: The false prophets who oppose Micah object because they assume that as "God's People," they will always live in His favor and protection. What is God's answer to this doctrine of "A loving God only"?

- God's answer begins in the second half of verse 7. Upright people will live in God's favor, but that is based on their genuine faith, not their genealogy.
- So, He says in v. 8-9, their claims to God are shredded by their ungodly actions. It is their behavior that is causing God's punishment to come to all the people.

<u>Group Discussion</u>: The "incurable wound" in 1:9 and the defilement beyond all remedy in 2:10 that has ruined the city of God requires drastic surgery by God. Remember, though, that there were still upright, godly people in the city who would also be swept up in the exile and punishment of His people. We may suffer in some way for other's sins, even though we are not at fault. Have you ever seen that happen? If so, how?

Much of the book of Micah is a disgusted condemnation of the corruption among the leaders, prophets and priests in both Israel and Judah. He warns that these leaders will face justice, and these prophets will "go dark" with no word from God. Micah uses images of cannibalism in Micah 3:1-3 to describe the way these unjust, opportunistic leaders consume and destroy the oppressed and poor of the nation. Here is a sampling of just how corrupt things have become:

Micah 3:5 (NIV)
[5] *This is what the Lord says: "As for the prophets who lead my people astray, they proclaim 'peace' if they have something to eat, but prepare to wage war against anyone*
who refuses to feed them.

Micah 3:11 (NIV)
[11] *Her leaders judge for a bribe, her priests teach for a price, and her prophets tell fortunes for money. Yet they look for the Lord's support and say, "Is not the Lord among us? No disaster will come upon us."*

Group Discussion: Based on these passages, what is the real motivation, the real god for these leaders?

- They act pious, but their real motivation is money. Micah clearly shows why they should not expect salvation from God: they use religion, but their hearts are nowhere near God.

What's the use of being righteous?

We've discussed the internal corruption that was rotting the nation from within. Let's look now at the external pressures – in the Assyrian threat – that was also at play in the time of Micah.

Micah 2:12-13 (NIV)

12 *"I will surely gather all of you, O Jacob;*
I will surely bring together the remnant of Israel.
I will bring them together like sheep in a pen,like a flock in its pasture;
the place will throng with people.
13 *One who breaks open the way will go up before them;*
they will break through the gate and go out.
Their king will pass through before them,
the Lord at their head."

Some writers think this describes the conditions in Jerusalem around 701 B.C. Refugees flooded in from Israel after the Assyrians conquered the northern kingdom in 722. More refugees came from Judah as Sennacherib swept over that country. Archeological records indicate the population of Jerusalem may have swelled to four times its previous size after the fall of the northern kingdom. And with the Assyrian army approaching the gates of Jerusalem, the people are crammed inside its walls like sheep in a pen.

We're going to leave the text of Micah for a while now to further explore the Assyrian threat. Hezekiah was on the throne in Jerusalem. He was a righteous king who endured a lot of resistance and scorn as he attempted to reform the corrupt religious and social conditions of Judah after the fall of Israel. He did what was right in God's eyes, yet he still saw almost his entire country overtaken by the cruel Assyrians.

2 Chronicles 32:1 (NIV)

After all that Hezekiah had so faithfully done, Sennacherib king of Assyria came and invaded Judah. He laid siege to the fortified cities, thinking to conquer them for himself.

According to Sennacherib's records, he took 46 walled cities, and countless unwalled cities, in Judea, which really left only Jerusalem standing. He also took 200,000 captives (Keathley 4). This would have included Micah's hometown of Moresheth, near the fortress of Lachish. In the ruins of the Assyrian palace in Nineveh (modern Iraq), a relief was found of the fall of the Lachish, including graphic pictures of Jews impaled on poles, skinned alive, beheaded, or carried into exile (Keathley 2). It is very likely some of Micah's own family were either prisoners, exiles, or dead at the hands of the Assyrians as he preached in the pressure cooker that was Jerusalem.

Group Discussion: Put yourself in Hezekiah's shoes. What would your prayers be like? What considerations, what options, would you weigh as you decided whether or not to surrender to the Assyrians?

When the Assyrians showed up surrounding Jerusalem, backed by an army, they began a campaign of propaganda and intimidation. As we read 2 Kings 18, it is easy to understand how this war machine could conquer so many nations. They were masters of psychological warfare.

2 Kings 18:17-35 (NIV)
17 The king of Assyria sent his supreme commander, his chief officer and his field commander with a large army, from Lachish
to King Hezekiah at Jerusalem. They came up to Jerusalem and stopped at the aqueduct of the Upper Pool, on the road to the
Washerman's Field. 18 They called for the king; and Eliakim son of Hilkiah the palace administrator, Shebna the secretary,
and Joah son of Asaph the recorder went out to them.
19 The field commander said to them, "Tell Hezekiah:
"'This is what the great king, the king of Assyria, says: On what are you basing this confidence of yours? 20 You say you have
strategy and military strength—but you speak only empty words. On whom are you depending, that you rebel against me? 21
Look now, you are depending on Egypt, that splintered reed of a staff, which pierces a man's hand and wounds him if he leans
on it! Such is Pharaoh king of Egypt to all who depend on him. 22 And if you say to me, "We are depending on the Lord our
God"—isn't he the one whose high places and altars Hezekiah removed, saying to Judah and Jerusalem, "You must worship
before this altar in Jerusalem"?
23 "'Come now, make a bargain with my master, the king of Assyria: I will give you two thousand horses—if you can put
riders on them! 24 How can you repulse one officer of the least of my master's officials, even though you are depending on Egypt
for chariots and horsemen? 25 Furthermore, have I come to attack and destroy this place without word from the Lord? The Lord
himself told me to march against this country and destroy it.'"
26 Then Eliakim son of Hilkiah, and Shebna and Joah said to the field commander, "Please speak to your servants in
Aramaic, since we understand it. Don't speak to us in Hebrew in the hearing of the people on the wall."
27 But the commander replied, "Was it only to your master and you that my master sent me to say these things, and not to the
men sitting on the wall—who, like you, will have to eat their own filth and drink their own urine?"
28 Then the commander stood and called out in Hebrew: "Hear the word of the great king, the king of Assyria! 29 This is what
the king says: Do not let Hezekiah deceive you. He cannot deliver you from my hand. 30 Do not let Hezekiah persuade you to
trust in the Lord when he says, 'The Lord will surely deliver us; this city will not be given into the hand of the king of Assyria.'
31 "Do not listen to Hezekiah. This is what the king of Assyria says: Make peace with me and come out to me. Then every one
of you will eat from his own vine and fig tree and drink water from his own cistern, 32 until I come and take you to a land like
your own, a land of grain and new wine, a land of bread and vineyards, a land of olive trees and honey. Choose life and not
death!
"Do not listen to Hezekiah, for he is misleading you when he says, 'The Lord will deliver us.' 33 Has the god of any nation ever
delivered his land from the hand of the king of Assyria? 34 Where are the gods of Hamath and Arpad? Where are the gods of
Sepharvaim, Hena and Ivvah? Have they rescued Samaria from my hand? 35 Who of all the gods of these countries has been
able to save his land from me? How then can the Lord deliver Jerusalem from my hand?"

<u>Group Discussion:</u> Do any of the Assyrian arguments sound similar to messages we hear today? How does Satan use some of the same psychological warfare and reasoning on us?

- How do you think you can overcome this temptation if you have never been able to before?
- Why are you resisting this when no one else is? If everyone is doing it, how can it be so bad?
- Look at all the wickedness and suffering that God has not been able to prevent. Why continue to hope in a God that allows cruelty and cancer and injustice?

The choice required of Hezekiah and the people of Jerusalem was between being practical and being faithful. For generations, the Israelites had been acculturated to the practices of their neighbors instead of being a counterculture. Instead of relying on God, they depended on military advances, alliances, money and intrigue for their security. Their society as a whole was ruled by pragmatism (VanGemeren 152). They did what felt natural, what looked easiest, what was best for them.

Surrounded by Assyrians, the rest of the country filled with Assyrians, with a chance now to either surrender and avoid bloodshed or fight against a vastly superior enemy, the practical option was obvious. The faithful option, to trust God and fight, did not look very practical.

<u>Group Discussion:</u> Would you agree that being faithful is often impractical? Describe some actions or decisions you have made in the name of faith that were very impractical.

- Stopping and praying for guidance instead of just getting busy with what we think is best seems impractical. It feels like we are wasting time because we are "too busy to pray".
- The command to sacrifice first fruits was very impractical. God required His people to give Him the first and best of their crops and herds. They had to give away what they normally would keep, and then trust God to provide after that. This flies in the face of modern financial advice to "pay yourself first."
- Many of the teachings in the Sermon on the Mount - turn the other cheek; love your enemies and do good to those who hate you; if someone forces you to go one mile, go with him two - are all "impractical" and counter to our instincts. None of those actions are the easiest options available in those situations.

And what does the Lord require of you?

Chapter 6 is organized like a court trial. It is God putting His people on trial as they ask Him why they are now in this position. Normally, judicial cases were heard at the city gates by the elders, but God calls the mountains to be the witnesses to this hearing.

Micah 6:1-8 (NIV)

Listen to what the Lord says: "Stand up, plead your case before the mountains; let the hills hear what you have to say.
2 *Hear, O mountains, the Lord's accusation; listen, you everlasting foundations of the earth. For the Lord has a case against his people; he is lodging a charge against Israel.*
3 *"My people, what have I done to you? How have I burdened you? Answer me.*
4 *I brought you up out of Egypt and redeemed you from the land of slavery. I sent Moses to lead you, also Aaron and Miriam.*
5 *My people, remember what Balak king of Moab counseled and what Balaam son of Beor answered. Remember your journey from Shittim to Gilgal, that you may know the righteous acts of the Lord."*

God is recounting His history of faithfulness to prove that He has always wanted to bless them, and proved that by delivering them from slavery. Balak was a Moabite king that hired the prophet Balaam to curse the Israelites, but Balaam kept blessing them because that is what God wanted to do (Numbers 22-24). God has always been motivated by love and the desire to bless His people. Even when they broke their covenant with Him by idol worship in Shittim (Numbers 25:1-9), He renewed the covenant with their children in Gilgal (Joshua 5:9).

But what God has always desired is that His people seek Him, and that they love what He loves – truth and holiness and justice. He is impressed with sincere hearts and sincere love in action, not empty religious rituals.

Verses 6-7 of chapter 6 are a series of rhetorical questions showing the futility of impressing God with only the rituals of worship, no matter how extravagant.

6 *With what shall I come before the Lord and bow down before the exalted God? Shall I come before him with burnt offerings, with calves a year old?*

[7] Will the Lord be pleased with thousands of rams, with ten thousand rivers of oil? Shall I offer my firstborn for my transgression, the fruit of my body for the sin of my soul?

Micah answers in verse 8 that God wants simple good behavior that reflects belief in a good God. This is what has been missing, and this is still, in the midst of the crisis of corruption and war, all that God wants from them.

[8] He has showed you, O man, what is good. And what does the Lord require of you? To act justly and to love mercy and to walk humbly with your God.

<u>Group Discussion:</u> Jesus said something very similar in Matthew 23:23, urging the Pharisees to not neglect the weightier matters of the Law: justice, mercy and faithfulness. What are some of the most memorable or powerful ways you have seen individual Christians or a congregation follow these teachings and show justice, mercy, or humility/faithfulness?

In chapter 7 is a personal statement from Micah about why he is hoping against hope in the midst of this horrible times. And then beginning in verse 8, he speaks for the entire nation of Israel and acts as their voice to their enemies.

Micah 7:7-10 (NIV)
[7] But as for me, I watch in hope for the Lord, I wait for God my Savior; my God will hear me.
[8] Do not gloat over me, my enemy! Though I have fallen, I will rise. Though I sit in darkness, the Lord will be my light.
[9] Because I have sinned against him, I will bear the Lord's wrath, until he pleads my case and establishes my right. He will bring me out into the light; I will see his righteousness.
[10] Then my enemy will see it and will be covered with shame, she who said to me,
"Where is the Lord your God?" My eyes will see her downfall; even now she will be trampled underfoot like mire in the streets.

And now for . . . the rest of the story

Faced with the choice of being practical or being "impractically faithful", King Hezekiah chose faith. He did not surrender, so Sennacherib's messengers returned to report to him in Lacish while the army no doubt stayed encamped around Jerusalem. Sennacherib sent a second message to Hezekiah, again scoffing at the Israelite God's ability to hold off the Assyrian army, who had just wiped out the second largest city in Judah and was now coming with full force to Jerusalem. Hezekiah spread this letter before the Lord and prayed.

2 Kings 19:15-19 (NIV)
[15] And Hezekiah prayed to the Lord: "O Lord, God of Israel, enthroned between the cherubim, you alone are God over all the kingdoms of the earth. You have made heaven and earth. [16] Give ear, O Lord, and hear; open your eyes, O Lord, and see; listen to the words Sennacherib has sent to insult the living God.
[17] "It is true, O Lord, that the Assyrian kings have laid waste these nations and their lands. [18] They have thrown their gods into the fire and destroyed them, for they were not gods but only wood and stone, fashioned by men's hands. [19] Now, O Lord our God, deliver us from his hand, so that all kingdoms on earth may know that you alone, O Lord, are God."

In response to Hezekiah's prayer, Isaiah delivers this response from God:

2 Kings 19:32-36 (NIV)
[32] "Therefore this is what the Lord says concerning the king of Assyria: "He will not enter this city or shoot an arrow here. He will not come before it with shield or build a siege ramp against it.
[33] By the way that he came he will return; he will not enter this city, declares the Lord.

[34] I will defend this city and save it, for my sake and for the sake of David my servant."
[35] That night the angel of the Lord went out and put to death a hundred and eighty-five thousand men in the Assyrian camp. When the people got up the next morning—there were all the dead bodies! [36] So Sennacherib king of Assyria broke camp and withdrew. He returned to Nineveh and stayed there.

Just like Micah promised in 7:10, the people of Jerusalem, trapped like sheep in a pen, see firsthand the destruction of their enemies. They wake to 185,000 dead Assyrians lying outside the city, a miracle of "impractical" faith.

A Future King

In the midst of that siege, when Hezekiah and his people were trapped by the awful military might of the Assyrians, and Hezekiah was bearing their insults, Micah delivers an enticing prophecy of another future king:

Micah 5:1-6 (NIV)
Marshal your troops now, city of troops, for a siege is laid against us.
They will strike Israel's ruler on the cheek with a rod.
2 *"But you, Bethlehem Ephrathah, though you are small among the clans of Judah,*
out of you will come for me one who will be ruler over Israel,
whose origins are from of old, from ancient times."
3 *Therefore Israel will be abandoned until the time when she who is in labor bears a son,*
and the rest of his brothers return to join the Israelites.
4 *He will stand and shepherd his flock in the strength of the Lord,*
in the majesty of the name of the Lord his God.
And they will live securely, for then his greatness
will reach to the ends of the earth.
5 *And he will be our peace when the Assyrians invade our land*
and march through our fortresses.
We will raise against them seven shepherds, even eight commanders,
6 *who will rule the land of Assyria with the sword, the land of Nimrod with drawn sword.*
He will deliver us from the Assyrians when they invade our land
and march across our borders.

<u>Group Discussion:</u> Who is this king? What are the clues to his identity in this passage?

- This is a messianic prophecy of Jesus.
- (verse 2) He is from Bethlehem and "from ancient times", implying he is eternal.
- (verse 4) Jesus was the good shepherd.

Micah, in this same prophecy, also makes clear that this future king would rule over a very different Israel:

Micah 5:10-15 (NIV)
[10] "In that day," declares the Lord, "I will destroy your horses from among you and demolish your chariots.
[11] I will destroy the cities of your land and tear down all your strongholds.
[12] I will destroy your witchcraft and you will no longer cast spells.
[13] I will destroy your idols and your sacred stones from among you; you will no longer bow down to the work of your hands.
[14] I will uproot from among you your Asherah poles when I demolish your cities.
[15] I will take vengeance in anger and wrath on the nations that have not obeyed me."

<u>Group Discussion:</u> **Why does God say that the first thing He will do for the renewal of the nation under this future king is to destroy their military might ("I will remove your horses from you and wreck your chariots. I will . . . tear down all your fortresses.")?**

- What they are about to witness with the miraculous defeat of Sennacherib's army overnight is that they cannot and should not trust in military might. God had always told Israel that He would fight for them and protect them, and warned them against entangling treaties with other nations, or in depending on their own might.
- Besides, Christ's kingdom would "not be of this world" and would not require traditional means like armies for advancing its cause.

The other step in the renewal of the nation would be the destruction of idolatry. This was indeed achieved, but not until the drastic discipline of exile finally broke the Hebrews' weakness for idolatry. After the exile, the Jews never again were tempted towards idol worship. They had other issues and failures, but after the exile, idol worship was not one of them.

8
NAHUM
God is good and angry

Jonah, Micah, and Nahum all prophesied during the reign of terror caused by Assyria, the ruthless, arrogant nation that dominated the Middle East at that time.

1. **Jonah – God gives Assyria a chance to change.**
   - Even 50 years before Jonah, Assyria had been threatening Israel. Jonah preached to the Assyrians in Nineveh, calling them to repent of their brutal arrogance. They did, briefly, but were soon back to the business of swallowing nations.
2. **Micah – Because Israel refuses to change, God uses the Assyrians to punish Israel.**
   - It was probably about 50 years after Jonah that the prophet Micah watched the Assyrians destroy Samaria, the capital city of Israel, and carry off thousands of Israelites into exile. They then captured and pillaged most of Judah, coming to the very gates of Jerusalem..
3. **Nahum – Because Assyria has not changed, God punishes them.**
   - Nahum painted a graphic picture of the destruction of Nineveh, which happened in 612 B.C., 110 years after the Assyrians tore through Israel and Judah.

We know very little about the person of Nahum, and we cannot date precisely when he lived. There are two events he mentions that help us narrow down his time frame, however. He mentions the defeat of the Egyptian city of Thebes in 663 B.C. after it has already happened. He also predicts the fall of Nineveh as a future event. Nineveh was destroyed in 612 B.C., so we know that Nahum prophesied sometime between 663 and 612 B.C.

In a sense, the exact date of this prophecy is not essential because it has a message that transcends a specific place or time. This book works on two levels. Nineveh in history is symbolic of all evil people in eternity. In other words, what God does to Nineveh He will do to all proud or cruel people on this earth. Nineveh's fate is the eventual fate of all evil on earth.

God is *angry*

Nahum 1:2-6 (NIV)

2 The Lord is a jealous and avenging God;
the Lord takes vengeance and is filled with wrath.
The Lord takes vengeance on his foes
and maintains his wrath against his enemies.
3 The Lord is slow to anger and great in power;

the Lord will not leave the guilty unpunished.
His way is in the whirlwind and the storm,
and clouds are the dust of his feet.
4 *He rebukes the sea and dries it up;*
he makes all the rivers run dry.
Bashan and Carmel wither
and the blossoms of Lebanon fade.
5 *The mountains quake before him*
and the hills melt away.
The earth trembles at his presence,
the world and all who live in it.
6 *Who can withstand his indignation?*
Who can endure his fierce anger?
His wrath is poured out like fire;
the rocks are shattered before him.

Group Discussion: These verses say God is what? How is he described? [Write on the board two columns with the same heading over both: "God is:________." then fill in the first column with answers from class]

- Jealous
- Filled with wrath
- Slow to anger
- Great in power

The book starts by describing God as jealous and angry. This idea of a jealous God is echoed several times in scripture. In **Exodus 34:14 (NIV),** God's very name is Jealous: *"Do not worship any other god, for the Lord, whose name is Jealous, is a jealous God."*

Group Discussion: What does it mean that God is jealous? Why does God emphasize His jealousy?

- There is one thing that God does not automatically own and will not take by force – our hearts. He jealously wants our hearts, our devotion, our commitment to Him – and He wants that because of His love for us, for our own good.
- When we are in love with something else besides God, we can't fully receive His love. When we are not in Him, given to Him, we are in danger of being lost to sin and death, but God gives us free will to make that choice.

God is good ***and*** angry

Nahum 1:7-8 (NIV)
7 *The Lord is good, a refuge in times of trouble.*
He cares for those who trust in him,
8 *but with an overwhelming flood*
he will make an end of Nineveh;
he will pursue his foes into darkness.

<u>Group Discussion:</u> These verses say God is what? How is he described? [write on board under second column titled "God is:________." answers from class]

- Good
- A refuge
- caring

After painting a vivid picture of the terrible power of an angry God, Nahum abruptly says God is good and caring, even though in the very next verse he describes how God will savagely "pursue his foes into darkness." We need to spend some time talking about this dichotomy because it is essential to our understanding of the nature of God, the nature of holiness, and the nature of sin.

<u>Group Discussion:</u> How do you reconcile these two "faces" of the same God? Does God have a split personality?

- Good people get angry at injustice. Good people all agree that evil needs to be stopped. At some point, evil has to be judged and punished, or we will always be held hostage in some way by bad people, always paying a price for the sins of others, our freedom and our happiness always vulnerable to others' selfishness.
- But just like good people get angry, a good God will also get angry. A good, loving God is sometimes filled with wrath, not despite but because of His love and goodness. If you don't oppose evil, then you can't call yourself good. If you love someone and you see them being hurt, you get angry about that. If that person you love is destroying herself, you get angry at her. If you didn't, if you did nothing when a loved one was being ruined, then you can't say you really love her.
- If God were not angry at wickedness, and if He allowed evil to continue forever, unpunished, that God would not be worthy of our worship. Even while we still live in a damaged world held hostage by sin, we are promised He will not let evil forever hold good hostage. There will be justice.
- **2 Thessalonians 1:6-7 (NIV)** *6 God is just: He will pay back trouble to those who trouble you 7 and give relief to you who are troubled, and to us as well. This will happen when the Lord Jesus is revealed from heaven in blazing fire with his powerful angels.*

If God is holy all the way – and holy means completely perfect and good and pure – then we can trust Him all the way, all the way to the gates of Hell. We can trust that whoever He decides to put on the other side of those gates was judged fairly and is there for the right reasons.

You can trust that he <u>loves</u> every one of us.

- **2 Peter 3:9 (NIV)** *9 The Lord is not slow in keeping his promise, as some understand slowness. He is patient with you, not wanting anyone to perish, but everyone to come to repentance.*

You can trust that He <u>knows the hearts</u> of each of us. He knows what's in our hearts better than even we do. He knows the chances we had and the decisions we made, and the reasons why.

- **1 Corinthians 4:4-5 (NIV)** *It is the Lord who judges me . . . He will bring to light what is hidden in darkness and will expose the motives of men's hearts. At that time each will receive his praise from God.*

You can trust His <u>judgment</u>.

- **Psalm 7:11a (ESV)** *God is a righteous judge*

<u>Group Discussion:</u> Some people respond that what we see in writings like Nahum's is the personality of God before Christ came; that there was an "Old Testament God" who is now kinder and gentler. Do you agree?

- God's anger is not a thing of the past. It appears numerous times in the New Testament.

- **Romans 2:5 (NIV)** *[5] But because of your stubbornness and your unrepentant heart, you are storing up wrath against yourself for the day of God's wrath, when his righteous judgment will be revealed.*
- **John 3:36** *[36] Whoever believes in the Son has eternal life, but whoever rejects the Son will not see life, for God's wrath remains on him."*

Nahum is a series of judgment oracles, taunts, and woes with a militaristic theme. Unlike Jonah, Nahum is not warning the Assyrians so they will repent. He is pronouncing their fate and describing their imminent destruction. While the prophecy is leveled against Nineveh, it's message also brings reassurance to Judah.

Nahum 1:12-15 (NIV)
[12] This is what the Lord says:
"Although they have allies and are numerous,
they will be cut off and pass away.
Although I have afflicted you, O Judah,
I will afflict you no more.
[13] Now I will break their yoke from your neck
and tear your shackles away."
[14] The Lord has given a command concerning you, Nineveh:
"You will have no descendants to bear your name.
I will destroy the carved images and cast idols
that are in the temple of your gods.
I will prepare your grave,
for you are vile."
[15] Look, there on the mountains,
the feet of one who brings good news,
who proclaims peace!
Celebrate your festivals, O Judah,
and fulfill your vows.
No more will the wicked invade you;
they will be completely destroyed.

<u>Group Discussion:</u> Remember we said that the terrifying destruction of Nineveh was symbolic of what would happen to all kingdoms and all people who do not respect and obey God. So the destruction of Nineveh is the preview of God's judgment on the entire world. As Christians, we eagerly await God's coming because it will bring us heaven, but that same coming will also bring terror and eternal death to untold millions of souls. When we echo Jesus' prayer in Matthew 6 and say, "Your kingdom come; your will be done on earth as it is in heaven," is this what we are asking for?

- John Mark Hicks writes of Matthew 6:10, "[these statements] fundamentally appeal for God to act . . . they are an identification of our will with God's will. It is our investment in the cause of God. It is our declaration that God's designs, his purposes, and his goals are our own . . . It is the submission of our desires and priorities to that of God's" (Hicks, *Theology).*

Play-by-play of the beating of a bully

In chapters two and three, Nahum gives us a collage of graphic images and sound bites of the coming fall of Nineveh. His vision reads like a movie script, and it proves to be very accurate historically.

Nineveh was located near the east bank of the Tigris river by modern city of Mosul in Iraq. The river acted as the western and southern boundaries of the city. A wall with 15 gates extended for eight miles. The city was about three miles wide and eight miles long inside the walls, but there were suburbs that extended 14 miles north and 20 miles south. It was a huge place and very well fortified. Here is what the two-month siege and fall of Nineveh looked and sounded like in the vision of Nahum:

Nahum 2:1-10 (NIV)

An attacker advances against you, Nineveh. Guard the fortress, watch the road, brace yourselves, marshal all your strength!
2 *The Lord will restore the splendor of Jacob like the splendor of Israel, though destroyers have laid them waste and have ruined their vines.*
3 *The shields of his soldiers are red; the warriors are clad in scarlet. The metal on the chariots flashes on the day they are made ready; the spears of pine are brandished.*
4 *The chariots storm through the streets, rushing back and forth through the squares. They look like flaming torches; they dart about like lightning.*
5 *He summons his picked troops, yet they stumble on their way. They dash to the city wall; the protective shield is put in place.*
6 *The river gates are thrown open and the palace collapses.*
7 *It is decreed that the city be exiled and carried away. Its slave girls moan like doves and beat upon their breasts.*
8 *Nineveh is like a pool, and its water is draining away. "Stop! Stop!" they cry, but no one turns back.*
9 *Plunder the silver! Plunder the gold! The supply is endless, the wealth from all its treasures!*
10 *She is pillaged, plundered, stripped! Hearts melt, knees give way, bodies tremble, every face grows pale.*

While the Babylonians, Medes and Scythians surrounded the city, the Khosr River flooded, perhaps because the attackers manipulated the floodgates, and broke down part of the wall. This fulfilled Nahum's prophesy in 1:8; 2:6 and 3:13 when he talked about "an overwhelming flood" and "the river gates are thrown open and the palace collapses." According to the ancient historian Diodorus Siculus, there was so much loot that the invaders did not pursue the fleeing Assyrian army. Instead, they started grabbing everything they could. This was described by Nahum in 2:8-10: "Plunder the silver! Plunder the gold! The supply is endless, the wealth from all its treasures . . . "

The devastation of the city was overwhelming and complete and within several centuries the very location of the city was forgotten. In the 2nd century A.D. the Greek satirist Lucian commented: "Nineveh is so completely destroyed that it is no longer possible to say where it stood. Not a single trace of it remains." It remained lost until British archeologists unearthed it in 1840 (*Baker Encylopedia*).

Nahum 2:11-12 (NIV)

11 *Where now is the lions' den, the place where they fed their young,*
where the lion and lioness went, and the cubs, with nothing to fear?
12 *The lion killed enough for his cubs and strangled the prey for his mate,*
filling his lairs with the kill and his dens with the prey.

Group Discussion: What might this lion imagery signify?

- The lion was a symbol of royalty throughout the Middle East, such as the biblical "lion of Judah."
- On the walls of Nineveh were found numerous depictions of Assyrian kings on lion hunts or even killing lions with their bare hands. Nahum, as he does often in this book, turns things upside down. These Assyrian "lions" who had torn and strangled others and filled their lairs with the torn flesh of the nations they had devoured, are now not the hunters, but the hunted. God says in 2:13, *"I am against you . . . and the sword will devour your young lions."*

The book of Nahum is a passionate book, and so is its God. Listen to how God talks to the Ninevites:

Nahum 3:4-6 (NIV)
4 all because of the wanton lust of a harlot,
alluring, the mistress of sorceries,
who enslaved nations by her prostitution
and peoples by her witchcraft.
5 "I am against you," declares the Lord Almighty.
"I will lift your skirts over your face.
I will show the nations your nakedness
and the kingdoms your shame.
6 I will pelt you with filth,
I will treat you with contempt
and make you a spectacle.

Nahum 3:13 (NIV)
13 Look at your troops—
they are all women!
The gates of your land
are wide open to your enemies;
fire has consumed their bars.

Group Discussion: In sports vernacular, we would say this is "trash-talking." It sounds like a warrior taunting his enemy. This is tough, almost vulgar language. Does this sound like the holy, pure God of heaven to you? Why would God use this language when speaking to Nineveh?

- He speaks in this way because it is language they would understand. It is the same language they used to intimidate others.
- Read Isaiah's prophecy against the Assyrians in 2 Kings 19:20-28 when they surrounded Jerusalem and mocked and threatened King Hezekiah. God is using the same threats and taunts against them that the Assyrians used against His people and Him:
- God made clear through Isaiah that the Assyrians were mistakenly taking credit for what God had ordained and allowed for His purposes, and while He has used them, He will not tolerate their rage and insolence.
- God is hitting the arrogant, male-dominated Assyrians where it would hurt them most – in their pride.
- Before God, the bellicose, cruel Assyrians are exposed for what they truly are; before God's holiness, this is how repulsive our sin, our pride, our puny power become.

Nahum is a unblinking statement of justice, of the old adage that what goes around, comes around. God compares Nineveh to a whore, that attracts others with her power and wealth, but who is never loved. When the end finally comes for her, He says in **Nahum 3:7**, "*Who will grieve for her? Where shall I seek comforters for you?*" In Nahum 3:10, God describes what Assyria did to the occupants of the Egyptian city of Thebes:

Nahum 3:10 (NIV)
10 Yet she was taken captive and went into exile.
Her infants were dashed to pieces at every street corner.
Lots were cast for her nobles, and all her great men were put in chains.

The implication is that the same will now be done to the inhabitants of Nineveh. The book ends with a rhetorical question:

Nahum 3:19 (NIV)
[19] *Nothing can heal you;*
your wound is fatal.
All who hear the news about you
clap their hands at your fall,
for who has not felt
your endless cruelty?

After centuries of brutal domination and aggressive plundering and intentional cruelty, what other fate can be expected, what other fate can be justified, except for Nineveh to fall in the same way? Since Assyria has visited only endless cruelty on everyone around it, who would come to its aid?

Group Discussion: The warning in Nahum is a timeless principle. It is one example of the truth in Galatians 6:7 (NIV) [7] ***Do not be deceived: God cannot be mocked. A man reaps what he sows.*** **Why do people or leaders or nations think they will be the exception to this rule?**

9
HABAKKUK
Unholy tools in holy hands

The three previous prophets we have discussed – Jonah, Micah, and Nahum – were all focused on the threat of the Assyrian Empire, which destroyed the northern kingdom of Israel and its capitol city Samaria in 722 B.C. Habakkuk and the prophetic books that follow will all be dealing with the threat from the Babylonian Empire against the southern kingdom of Judah.

Although it is not possible to date precisely from internal evidence, Habakkuk probably lived during the reigns of King Josiah and King Jehoikim. If that is true, he saw the fall of Assyria in 612 B.C. and the rise of Babylon as the next great threat to Judah. More locally, he saw the sudden death of Josiah, which ended that king's attempt to reform Judah and wipe out idol worship. Jehoikim, a selfish, godless king took over in Jerusalem, and Judah rapidly lost its independence politically and its soul religiously. Habakkuk prophesied during the same time as Jeremiah, the weeping prophet that watched the sad twilight of God's people before Jerusalem fell to Babylon in 586 B.C.

Group Discussion: This is a somewhat unique book in that we overhear the prophet question God. Can you think of some other Bible characters who questioned or debated God?

- Moses reasoned with God more than once to talk Him out of destroying the Israelites.
- Job repeatedly demanded answers from God and challenged Him to explain Himself.
- Jeremiah wrestled with God intellectually and emotionally.
- Even the human side of Jesus wrestled with God's will in the Garden of Gethsemane: "If it is your will, let this cup pass from me."

How long, O Lord

The first question Habakkuk asks of God is the paradox of why God does not intervene in the rampant wickedness and injustice in Judah. How long, he asks, before God shows up and does something?

Habakkuk 1:2-4 (NIV)
2 *How long, O Lord, must I call for help,*
but you do not listen?
Or cry out to you, "Violence!"
but you do not save?

[3] Why do you make me look at injustice?
Why do you tolerate wrong?
Destruction and violence are before me;
there is strife, and conflict abounds.
[4] Therefore the law is paralyzed,
and justice never prevails.
The wicked hem in the righteous,
so that justice is perverted.

<u>Group Discussion:</u> Are there things happening in the world now that invoke the same feelings in you? What current events, injustices, etc. make you wonder why God has not yet intervened? Why do you think God would allow such a thing to continue?

- **2 Peter 3:15 (NIV)** [15] Bear in mind that our Lord's patience means salvation, just as our dear brother Paul also wrote you with the wisdom that God gave him.
- **Romans 2:4 (NIV)** [4] Or do you show contempt for the riches of his kindness, forbearance and patience, not realizing that God's kindness is intended to lead you to repentance?
- This has been a struggle for saints all through the Bible. Look at Psalm 6:2-7, Psalm 13:1-2, and Revelation 6:9-11 for other times when humans were forced to wait on God's justice, not understanding God's timing while wickedness seemingly continued unchecked.

Here is how God answers Habakkuk:

Habakkuk 1:5-11 (NIV)
[5] "Look at the nations and watch—
and be utterly amazed.
For I am going to do something in your days
that you would not believe,
even if you were told.
[6] I am raising up the Babylonians,
that ruthless and impetuous people,
who sweep across the whole earth
to seize dwelling places not their own.
[7] They are a feared and dreaded people;
they are a law to themselves
and promote their own honor.
[8] Their horses are swifter than leopards,
fiercer than wolves at dusk.
Their cavalry gallops headlong;
their horsemen come from afar.
They fly like a vulture swooping to devour;
[9] they all come bent on violence.
Their hordes advance like a desert wind
and gather prisoners like sand.
[10] They deride kings and scoff at rulers.
They laugh at all fortified cities;
they build earthen ramps and capture them.
[11] Then they sweep past like the wind and go on—
guilty men, whose own strength is their god."

Weeding the garden with a bulldozer

God's solution to the wickedness in Judah is to send the pagan, arrogant, brutal Babylonian army to swarm over Jerusalem, killing and imprisoning thousands of Habakkuk's people. This is indeed a surprising response to Habakkuk's prayers.

Group Discussion: Imagine that your church, dismayed by the lack of morality in the culture around you, begins to pray for God to revive the church and its influence on the culture. Soon after, a corrupt government comes into office, revokes religious freedoms, and even demolishes your church building while an economic depression causes many church members to lose their jobs and homes. Did God answer your prayers?

That is basically the future awaiting the righteous remnant of Judah. Habakkuk struggles with why God would use the unholy Babylonians as tools in His holy plan. There is no doubt this is God's plan. In Jeremiah 24:9, he calls Nebuchadnezzar, the Babylonian tyrant, "my servant." God actually tells His people through Jeremiah to submit to the Babylonians (Jer. 27:9-11; 29:4-9). In fact, He said if they did submit, they would live; if they fled, they would die. Understandably, this raises even more concerns for Habakkuk.

Habakkuk 1:12-17 (NIV)
12 *O Lord, are you not from everlasting?*
My God, my Holy One, we will not die.
O Lord, you have appointed them to execute judgment;
O Rock, you have ordained them to punish.
13 *Your eyes are too pure to look on evil;*
you cannot tolerate wrong.
Why then do you tolerate the treacherous?
Why are you silent while the wicked
swallow up those more righteous than themselves?
14 *You have made men like fish in the sea,*
like sea creatures that have no ruler.
15 *The wicked foe pulls all of them up with hooks,*
he catches them in his net,
he gathers them up in his dragnet;
and so he rejoices and is glad.
16 *Therefore he sacrifices to his net*
and burns incense to his dragnet,
for by his net he lives in luxury
and enjoys the choicest food.
17 *Is he to keep on emptying his net,*
destroying nations without mercy?

Group Discussion: What is Habakkuk questioning about God and His plan? What are his doubts?

- God, is what you are doing fair? Is it wise to fight evil with even more evil?
- Isn't this like weeding the garden with a bulldozer; isn't the cure worse than the disease?
- The Babylonians are even worse than we are. Why use them? Don't they need to be punished even more than we do?

<u>**Group Discussion:**</u> **How can unholy tools be used by God's holy hands? What other times or what other ways do you believe God has used wicked people or events for His purposes?**

<u>**Group Discussion:**</u> **How would you answer Habakkuk's question in verse 13 about the existence of evil under the very nose of the pure God? How do you explain how God can look upon or be in the presence of evil and remain holy?**

- <u>Evil is like a hole in the field of goodness</u>. Perhaps a good way to describe evil is to think of it as a hole in a field. A hole is not a "thing" but an absence of a thing. It is not an illusion though, for people can step in hole they do not see and twist their ankles. So if we say that all goodness comes from God, evil is a "hole" in that goodness; it is the absence of God's goodness. It is not a "thing" that God created, but it exists because His goodness exists.
- <u>Evil is like a shadow in God's light</u>. In other words, evil only becomes apparent in the presence of goodness. If a shadow is where light is blocked or reduced by an object, did the light or the object create the shadow? No object, no shadow. Yet, no light, no shadow either. Evil really exists, but evil does not have an existence independent of God who is light and the source of all goodness (Commentary on Hab. 1:13 on www.BibleQuery.org). Evil is not a part of God, but it does exist, ironically, because He exists.

<u>**Group Discussion:**</u> **Look again at 1:13, where Habakkuk asks God, "Why are you silent while the wicked swallow up those more righteous than themselves? " Do you think that is how God viewed the situation? Why or why not?**

- "More righteous" is a relative term. In truth, the Israelites were not righteous either. In fact, if you remember Amos, his point was that the Israelites were the worst of all the nations because they should have known better. Unlike the surrounding nations, they had a long relationship with God and knew His expectations (Keathley, Hab. 1:12-2:1).
- **Romans 3:9-10** (NIV): *[9] What shall we conclude then? Are we any better? Not at all! We have already made the charge that Jews and Gentiles alike are all under sin. [10] As it is written: "There is no one righteous, not even one . . . "*
- While we struggle with how God can tolerate sinful people, we rarely struggle with how God can tolerate us.

Habakkuk 2:1 (NIV)

I will stand at my watch
and station myself on the ramparts;
I will look to see what he will say to me,
and what answer I am to give to this complaint.

<u>**Group Discussion:**</u> **Although Habakkuk 2:1 almost gives the impression that the prophet is wincing as he waits for God's reaction to being questioned, God doesn't angrily rebuke Habakkuk for challenging or questioning Him. Any thoughts as to why not?**

- Perhaps most significant is Habakkuk's attitude. He asks these questions and then waits for an answer. Too often people get angry with God and turn their backs on Him. They don't want His answer, just the self-destructive satisfaction of telling Him off.

It looks good from a distance, but . . .

Habakkuk 2:4-20 is a series of "woes" against Babylon. In this section, God is actually taunting Babylon with these woes that are ironic parodies of a funeral dirge. In the original Hebrew, verses 6-14 and 15-20 were both 10 lines long, each ending with a contrasting statement between the ungodly Babylonians and God. Here are some excerpts from that section. After Habakkuk asks why the wicked are tolerated and seem to have it so good, God invites Habakkuk to look a little closer at the repercussions of being wicked.

Habakkuk 2:5-13 (NIV)

5 *indeed, wine betrays him; he is arrogant and never at rest.*
Because he is as greedy as the grave
and like death is never satisfied,
he gathers to himself all the nations
and takes captive all the peoples.
6 *"Will not all of them taunt him with ridicule and scorn, saying,*
"Woe to him who piles up stolen goods
and makes himself wealthy by extortion!
How long must this go on?'
7 *Will not your debtors suddenly arise?*
Will they not wake up and make you tremble?
Then you will become their victim.
8 *Because you have plundered many nations,*
the peoples who are left will plunder you.
For you have shed man's blood;
you have destroyed lands and cities and everyone in them.
9 *"Woe to him who builds his realm by unjust gain*
to set his nest on high,
to escape the clutches of ruin!
10 *You have plotted the ruin of many peoples,*
shaming your own house and forfeiting your life.
11 *The stones of the wall will cry out,*
and the beams of the woodwork will echo it.
12 *"Woe to him who builds a city with bloodshed*
and establishes a town by crime!
13 *Has not the Lord Almighty determined*
that the people's labor is only fuel for the fire,
that the nations exhaust themselves for nothing?

Group Discussion: What does God point out about the lifestyles of the Babylonians?

- The righteous lifestyle is its own reward. The sinful lifestyle is its own punishment. Greed is insatiable, and the greedy suffer the law of diminishing returns.
- They live in fear: fear of losing their stuff, fear of payback from those they have abused.
- Oppression cannot be maintained forever. Eventually, the people they mistreat will fight back.
- All the effort required to gain this material wealth is exhausting and pointless. The Babylonians cannot enjoy their homes because they are ashamed. The price they pay for this lifestyle is too high to justify it.
- See Psalm 37 for an extended discussion of why the wicked should not be envied and why righteousness is its own reward.

Thanks for nothing

In chapter 3, Habakkuk words a prayer that accepts God's ways, that acknowledges His power, and that shows the prophet has come to terms with the fact that Babylon will indeed invade Jerusalem. Habakkuk also promises to "wait patiently for the day of calamity to come on the nation invading us." He knows that even though Babylon is the unholy tool currently being used by God, Babylon's wickedness will not go unpunished. That is a big stretch of faith for any follower of God. And then Habakkuk makes an even more extraordinary statement in 3:17-18.

Habakkuk 3:17-19 (NIV)
17 *Though the fig tree does not bud*
and there are no grapes on the vines,
though the olive crop fails
and the fields produce no food,
though there are no sheep in the pen
and no cattle in the stalls,
18 *yet I will rejoice in the Lord,*
I will be joyful in God my Savior.
19 *The Sovereign Lord is my strength;*
he makes my feet like the feet of a deer,
he enables me to go on the heights.

No doubt this was the experience of many devout Jews when the Babylonians did come; their possessions were carried off, their means of survival were destroyed, they were hungry and homeless. Just like all their wicked neighbors, the righteous in Jerusalem were overwhelmed by the same injustices and losses. Yet, says the prophet, "I will rejoice in the Lord, I will be joyful in God." That's an extraordinary statement of unconditional faith regardless of circumstances. It is a sentiment expressed in several psalms as well.

Group Discussion: Read Psalm 13. We're not sure what was happening in David's life, or what he had been praying for when he wrote this, but obviously he is tired of waiting for an answer. Is there anything in this psalm that surprises you?

- David is obviously frustrated, and even angry, at God. He wants an answer.
- In verses 5 & 6 the tone changes drastically, with words like *trust, rejoice, deliverance,* and *sing.*
- But when David writes verses 5 and 6, his situation has not changed. It doesn't say that he has received his answer, and his enemies have disappeared. The words that bring him peace are future tense: my heart *will* rejoice; I *will* sing.
- This doesn't mean he knows exactly how that will happen through God, and it doesn't mean that God will do exactly what David hopes, but David trusts that God will do something that will bring a happy ending to this trial.
- David is still waiting at the end of this psalm, but he has remembered something that changes the wait. He has reminded himself that God can be trusted. David operates under the assumption that if he just trust in God, eventually his heart will rejoice, and he will be delivered, and he will sing because God will be generous.
- That reminder, and that trust in a future deliverance, work retroactively in a sense, back to where David is still waiting, but now he can wait with a different feeling, with a sense of peace and security.

Paul expressed the same unconditional faith in Philippians 4:4-7 (NIV)
4 Rejoice in the Lord always. I will say it again: Rejoice! 5 Let your gentleness be evident to all. The Lord is near. 6 Do not be anxious about anything, but in every situation, by prayer and petition, with thanksgiving, present your requests to God. 7 And the peace of God, which transcends all understanding, will guard your hearts and your minds in Christ Jesus.

Notice that Paul doesn't promise an answer, or that we will get all we expect or want, but what he does promise is peace, peace that passes understanding.

<u>Group Discussion:</u> I don't know what you are waiting for today, I don't know what unanswered prayer may be weighing on you right now, but consider if you knew that whatever does happen will be good in the end. If you knew that God may do something completely unexpected, that you may have to wait even longer, that it will turn out very differently that what you hoped, but in the end you will be very pleased and even rejoicing. How would that change the waiting in the meantime?

<u>Group Discussion:</u> A platitude we often hear when faced with unexpected tragedy or overwhelming burdens is this: "God will not give you more than you can bear." Do you agree with that statement? Why or why not?

Can you imagine a tipping point when losses or injustices or sorrows would be so great you could not remain faithful to God? Can you see yourself at a point where you would rather turn your back and forever stay angry at God? If that is the case, you value those things, those people, those expectations more than God. Not just God, actually, but also everything that comes only through Him – eternal life, purpose and meaning, forgiveness instead of wrath.

The message of Habakkuk is that there should be no tipping point. There is no place, no reason, no amount of glory or money that can replace God. We can question Him, we can wrestle with Him, He may break us, but we cannot escape or ignore or overpower Him. He will hammer on our hearts, invert our short-sighted expectations, and force us to be patient and malleable while we are near Him, but despite the pain and bewilderment that may come with that, our only good choice is to remain near Him.

10
ZEPHANIAH
The Singed Remnant

Zephaniah 1:1 (NIV)
The word of the Lord that came to Zephaniah son of Cushi, the son of Gedaliah, the son of Amariah, the son of Hezekiah, during the reign of Josiah son of Amon king of Judah:

Zephaniah the prophet and Josiah the king were both descended from King Hezekiah (Zephaniah's great-great grandfather, and Josiah's great grandfather), so Zephaniah may have had direct access to Josiah and helped influence the young king to begin a campaign of religious reform in Judah. Josiah became king at age eight after the assassination of his wicked father. He "began to seek the God of his father David" at age sixteen, and at twenty-years-old began to "purge Judah and Jerusalem of high places, Asherah poles, carved idols and cast images." Then when he was twenty-six, Josiah started the expensive project of repairing the temple. It is described in 2 Chronicles 34 as a "ruin." The condition of the temple was absolutely deplorable, not just because it was broken down, but because of what had been done inside it by Josiah's wicked father and grandfather.

2 Kings 23:4-7 (NIV)
4 The king [Josiah] ordered Hilkiah the high priest, the priests next in rank and the doorkeepers to remove from the temple of the Lord all the articles made for Baal and Asherah and all the starry hosts. He burned them outside Jerusalem in the fields of the Kidron Valley and took the ashes to Bethel. 5 He did away with the pagan priests appointed by the kings of Judah to burn incense on the high places of the towns of Judah and on those around Jerusalem—those who burned incense to Baal, to the sun and moon, to the constellations and to all the starry hosts. 6 He took the Asherah pole from the temple of the Lord to the Kidron Valley outside Jerusalem and burned it there. He ground it to powder and scattered the dust over the graves of the common people. 7 He also tore down the quarters of the male shrine prostitutes, which were in the temple of the Lord and where women did weaving for Asherah.

While repairing the temple, the workers made a profound discovery: the book of the Law (probably a copy of Deuteronomy). Judah had fallen so far away from God that the Mosaic Law had actually been lost! And it had been lost, in all places, in the temple!

Centuries before, in **Deuteronomy 17:18-20**, God had given a homework assignment to future kings: *18 When he takes the throne of his kingdom, he is to write for himself on a scroll a copy of this law, taken from that of the priests, who are Levites. 19 It is to be with him, and he is to read it all the days of his life so that he may learn to revere the Lord his God and follow carefully all the words of this law and these decrees 20 and not consider himself better than his brothers and turn from the law to the right or to the left. Then he and his descendants will reign a long time over his kingdom in Israel.*

Group Discussion: Each young king was to copy by hand the book of Deuteronomy, and then every day read from that personal copy of the Law. Obviously, none of Israel's kings had done their homework in a long time. What would this homework do for the young kings?

Josiah is absolutely devastated when he hears Deuteronomy because he realizes how far his nation has fallen from God's vision for it. He sends priests to the prophetess Huldah to see what he can do.

2 Chronicles 34:23-28 (NIV)
23 She said to them, "This is what the Lord, the God of Israel, says: Tell the man who sent you to me, 24 'This is what the
Lord says: I am going to bring disaster on this place and its people—all the curses written in the book that has been read in the
presence of the king of Judah. 25 Because they have forsaken me and burned incense to other gods and provoked me to anger by
all that their hands have made, my anger will be poured out on this place and will not be quenched.' 26 Tell the king of Judah,
who sent you to inquire of the Lord, 'This is what the Lord, the God of Israel, says concerning the words you heard: 27 Because
your heart was responsive and you humbled yourself before God when you heard what he spoke against this place and its people,
and because you humbled yourself before me and tore your robes and wept in my presence, I have heard you, declares the Lord.
28 Now I will gather you to your fathers, and you will be buried in peace. Your eyes will not see all the disaster I am going to
bring on this place and on those who live here.'"

Basically, she responds that it is too late. The die is cast. The cancer of idol worship and rebellion has spread so deep within the nation that it cannot be corrected without the drastic action of exile, which is among the curses Huldah referenced from **Deuteronomy 27:14-26 and 28:15-68**. But because his heart is right, the destruction of Judah will be postponed as long as Josiah is alive. For the rest of his reign, Josiah was obsessed with wiping out Israel's insidious idol worship.

2 Chronicles 34:31-33 (NIV)
31 The king stood by his pillar and renewed the covenant in the presence of the Lord—to follow the Lord and keep his commands, statutes and decrees with all his heart and all his soul, and to obey the words of the covenant written in this book.
32 Then he had everyone in Jerusalem and Benjamin pledge themselves to it; the people of Jerusalem did this in accordance with the covenant of God, the God of their ancestors.
33 Josiah removed all the detestable idols from all the territory belonging to the Israelites, and he had all who were present in Israel serve the Lord their God. As long as he lived, they did not fail to follow the Lord, the God of their fathers.

Group Discussion: If you read between the lines, it appears that Josiah treated this as a military campaign. He went to war against idolatry and imposed Yahweh worship on Judah, but not everyone shared his zeal. What has been your observation in situations where religious obedience was "forced" on someone? What is the typical response or result?

- Idol worship may have gone "underground," but because they went so quickly back to wickedness after Josiah's death (to see the decline just 30 years after Josiah's death, read 2 Chronicles 36:14-16), it is unlikely the people's repentance was ever complete or genuine. For this reason, the prophecy of Zephaniah could have come before Josiah's reforms, but it could also have come anytime during them.

If I've said it once, I've said it a thousand times!

Group Discussion: By this point, the people of Jerusalem have heard basically the same message from over a dozen prophets whose words are preserved in scripture, plus many others alluded to in scripture. These men and women have repeatedly delivered the same basic message of warnings and promises. Why did God continue to send prophet after prophet for three centuries? Why isn't saying it once enough?

- God loves His people, so He is patient and slow to anger and gives them every opportunity to change.
- Different voices reach different ears. With all the various personalities of the prophets, they each bring a different slant to the same message to appeal to different audiences.
- Humans tend to be nearsighted when it comes to history. We value what is new more than what is old. We like to think that our generation and our time is something special. We always think that we are on the edge of the Next Big Thing. Therefore we are more apt to pay attention to a prophet from our own generation versus a dead prophet from centuries ago.
- As parents, we are often flabbergasted that our children constantly test their boundaries. Every mom and dad has used the old line, "If I told you once, I've told you a thousand times!" No doubt that was God's frustration too as His people seemed determined to run headlong off the same cliff again and again. Yet He sent prophet after prophet to patiently try to turn the people around. By the time of Zephaniah, though, the warnings are especially ominous because now God has decided that things have gone too far. There is no turning back. Israel has already fallen, and now Judah is next.

Zephaniah 1:2-3 (NIV)
2 *"I will sweep away everything from the face of the earth," declares the Lord.*
3 *"I will sweep away both men and animals;*
I will sweep away the birds of the air
and the fish of the sea.
The wicked will have only heaps of rubble
when I cut off man from the face of the earth,"
declares the Lord.

Zephaniah 1:18 (NIV)
18 *Neither their silver nor their gold*
will be able to save them
on the day of the Lord's wrath."
In the fire of his jealousy
the whole earth will be consumed,
for he will make a sudden end
of all who live on the earth.

Group Discussion: What does Zephaniah make clear about the nature of the coming judgment?

- It will be complete and inescapable.
- The list of beings facing destruction, *men, animals, birds* and *fish,* shows that he proposes an act of 'un-creation'. These are listed in exactly the opposite order of their appearance in the original creation account in Gen. 1:20–28 (Carson, *New Bible Commentary*).
- By using the imagery of dismantling creation, God is saying that His judgment will be like tearing a house down to the foundation. There will be nothing that will not be exposed.

In some sections, Zephaniah focuses a series of judgment prophecies against Judah and Jerusalem, but in other places he is talking about a Day of punishment that is much wider in scope. Prophecies often exist on two planes:
1). The Immediate: the historical, earthly, or specific;
2) The Ultimate: the apocalyptic, spiritual, or universal.

Sometimes a prophecy also works on both levels simultaneously; what will happen to a specific people in history (destruction of Nineveh in 612 B.C.) will also happen to all wickedness for eternity when Christ returns. Both instances are described by the prophets as "The Day of the Lord."

In the following passage, Zephaniah specifies that this is an immediate prophecy about the future fate of Judah and Jerusalem.

Zephaniah 1:4-17 (NIV)

4 *"I will stretch out my hand against Judah and against all who live in Jerusalem.*
I will destroy every remnant of Baal worship in this place,
the very names of the idolatrous priests—
5 *those who bow down on the roofs to worship the starry host,*
those who bow down and swear by the Lord and who also swear by Molek,
6 *those who turn back from following the Lord and neither seek the Lord nor inquire of him."*
7 *Be silent before the Sovereign Lord, for the day of the Lord is near.*
The Lord has prepared a sacrifice; he has consecrated those he has invited.
8 *"On the day of the Lord's sacrifice I will punish the officials and the king's sons and all those clad*
in foreign clothes.
9 *On that day I will punish all who avoid stepping on the threshold,*
who fill the temple of their gods with violence and deceit.
10 *"On that day," declares the Lord,*
"a cry will go up from the Fish Gate, wailing from the New Quarter,
and a loud crash from the hills.
11 *Wail, you who live in the market district;*
all your merchants will be wiped out,
all who trade with silver will be destroyed.
12 *At that time I will search Jerusalem with lamps*
and punish those who are complacent,
who are like wine left on its dregs,
who think, 'The Lord will do nothing, either good or bad.'
13 *Their wealth will be plundered, their houses demolished.*
Though they build houses, they will not live in them;
though they plant vineyards, they will not drink the wine."
14 *The great day of the Lord is near— near and coming quickly.*
The cry on the day of the Lord is bitter;
the Mighty Warrior shouts his battle cry.
15 *That day will be a day of wrath—*
a day of distress and anguish, a day of trouble and ruin,
a day of darkness and gloom, a day of clouds and blackness—
16 *a day of trumpet and battle cry against the fortified cities*
and against the corner towers.
17 *"I will bring such distress on all people that they will grope about like those who are blind,*
because they have sinned against the Lord.
Their blood will be poured out like dust and their entrails like dung.

Group Discussion: Why is God angry at Judah? What are some things mentioned in 1:4-13?

Group Discussion: The most prevalent charge against them is idolatry. God meant for the destruction of the Temple and the ensuing exile to finally "cure" His people of idolatry. Why do you think idol worship was so appealing to these people for so long?

- The idols gave them something concrete and tangible to connect to, unlike the invisible God.
- Peer pressure was intense in cultures who attributed weather and fertility and victory in battle to appeasing fickle gods. If you were the only people in your community not worshipping that city's gods, and there was a natural disaster, then your neighbors would assume it was because you had angered the gods. Conformity to pagan rituals was seen as good citizenship.
- The worship of these gods could involve sexual pleasure, music, passionate rituals, and ecstatic parties, which had obvious attractions.
- Many of these cults were focused on agendas like increasing fertility, rather than imposing high moral standards.

From the time Moses led them out of Egypt, through the conquest of Canaan and the era of the judges and the monarchy, the Israelites had constantly been pulled away by the temptations of idol worship. The exile was the final, ultimate act to reset the Israelites relationship with their God based on the first of the Ten Commandments: "You shall have no other gods before me." This relationship would only work if that first commandment was respected.

Look up the word *idol* or *idolatry* in your Bible's concordance. In the major and minor prophets, the word appears dozens of times because it was such an insidious plague among God's people. In Ezra and Nehemiah and Malachi, written after the remnant of Judah returned to Jerusalem from Babylon and rebuilt the Temple, the word doesn't appear once.

In the rest of scripture written after the Babylonian captivity, idolatry is mentioned, but as something happening in other cultures, not among the Jews. It is an issue for Greek Christians and churches, but not among the Jews. The Jews continued to have many struggles, but worshipping wood and stone was not one of them. God's "cure did exactly what He intended.

The Remnant: the people of the future

<u>Group Discussion:</u> Does the word *remnant* have a positive or negative connotation for you? What do you associate with that word?

- Probably the most common synonym to remnant in our vernacular is *leftovers*. It is not a victorious word. At best it implies survival.
- In the prophets, it refers to who is left over after a catastrophe or purging.
- In the prophets, it is very desirable to be counted among the remnant. Zephaniah spends much of his time describing these people and how to be one.

The core message of Zephaniah is that there <u>will</u> be judgment, but there <u>can be</u> salvation. Sprinkled throughout these oracles of judgment are enticing promises that a remnant will come through God's judgment and live to be part of a blessed restoration. We're going to read through several of those promises, and as we do, pay attention to the common thread among the remnant, and what differentiates them from others.

Zephaniah 2:3 (NIV)

3 Seek the Lord, all you humble of the land, you who do what he commands. Seek righteousness, seek humility; perhaps you will be sheltered on the day of the Lord's anger.

Zephaniah 2:6-7 (NIV)

6 The land by the sea, where the Kerethites dwell, will be a place for shepherds and sheep pens.

[7] It will belong to the remnant of the house of Judah; there they will find pasture.
In the evening they will lie down in the houses of Ashkelon.
The Lord their God will care for them; he will restore their fortunes.

Zephaniah 2:9 (NIV)
[9] Therefore, as surely as I live,"
declares the Lord Almighty, the God of Israel,
"surely Moab will become like Sodom,
the Ammonites like Gomorrah—
a place of weeds and salt pits,
a wasteland forever.
The remnant of my people will plunder them;
the survivors of my nation will inherit their land."

Zephaniah 3:12-13 (NIV)
[12] But I will leave within you the meek and humble, who trust in the name of the Lord.
[3] The remnant of Israel will do no wrong; they will speak no lies, nor will deceit be found in their mouths. They will eat and lie down and no one will make them afraid."

Group Discussion: So, what were the characteristics common to the remnant? How was the line drawn between those who would be consumed and destroyed in the fiery Day of the Lord and those who would endure it but survive as the "singed remnant?"

- Zephaniah sees two groups of people: those who have a future (the remnant) and those who don't. Those who don't are described as being two-faced, bowing down to God and some other favorite god (1:5). Or they simply ignore God (1:6), and shamelessly do whatever they can get away with (3:1-5). The crucial difference between the two groups seems to be humility that is the product of a healthy fear of God.
- This parallels a statement Jesus made in the Sermon on the Mount in Matthew 5:5, "Blessed are the meek, for they will inherit the earth." Jesus was quoting from Psalm 37:11, which says, "But the meek will inherit the land and enjoy peace and prosperity."

Group Discussion: Why did Zephaniah focus on humility as the attribute most needed for the people he was preaching to?

- As we saw in Huldah's prophecy, God rewarded Josiah's humility by preserving the nation for his entire reign (2 Chronicles 34:27).
- Humility is also synonymous with a fear of God. These idolatrous people did not fear God or did not fear only God, and that was the critical sin that so insulted God.
- Humility leads to repentance of sin and dependence on God. Judah was sealed for destruction because they were not willing to listen to the prophets and humble themselves.

As with many prophets, Zephaniah ends on a hopeful note. Zephaniah 3:9-20 is a picture of unity and restoration that works on the immediate level – describing the return of the Jews from Babylonian exile – and on an ultimate level as a portrait of Heaven.

11
HAGGAI
Don't feed God leftovers

Here is a simple chart to help us place chronologically various events and characters that we will encounter in Haggai, Zechariah, and Malachi:

540 BC	530	520	510	500	490	480	470	460	450	440	430
Zerubbabel returns from exile, begins temple (536) Work stopped (534)		Work on temple resumes (520) Temple finished (516)						Ezra goes to Jerusalem (458)	Nehemiah goes to Jerusalem and rebuilds wall in 52 days (445)		
Ezra Chapters 1-6						**Esther 485-464**		**Ezra Chapters 7-10 (457)**	**Nehemiah (445 – 415)**		
		Haggai (520)								**Malachi? (dates uncertain)**	
		Zechariah (520-518)									
Daniel 605-536											

The downfall of Jerusalem that God had threatened for so long came at the hands of the Babylonians in three stages.

1. In 605 B.C., Nebuchadnezzar carried into captivity many of the most promising young men in Jerusalem, including Daniel.
2. in 598 B.C., Nebuchadnezzar took King Jehoichin and about 10,000 of the ruling class from Jerusalem to Babylon.
3. in 586 B.C., the Babylonians answered yet another rebellion by the Jews with total destruction of the temple and the city. All the Israelites except the poorest farmers were carried into exile (Willis 75).

But in the first stage of the exile, Jeremiah had promised that the Jews would return from exile in 70 years (Jer. 25:11-12). The 70 years can be added up in two ways:

1. The first wave of exiles departed Jerusalem in 605 B.C. and the first returnees came back 70 years later in 535 B.C.
2. The Temple was destroyed in 586 B.C., and the new one was completed 70 years later in 516 B.C.

Ezekiel prophesied that some of the Jews would return to Jerusalem, rebuild the city and the temple, restore worship, and redistribute the land to the tribes (Ezekiel 40-48). As predicted, the Babylonians fell to the Persians in 539 B.C., and Cyrus the Great, the new Persian leader, initiated a goodwill campaign by giving the exiles scattered throughout the Babylonian empire the opportunity to return to their native countries.

Ezra 1:1-5 (NIV)

In the first year of Cyrus king of Persia, in order to fulfill the word of the Lord spoken by Jeremiah, the Lord moved the heart of Cyrus king of Persia to make a proclamation throughout his realm and also to put it in writing:
2 "This is what Cyrus king of Persia says:
"The Lord, the God of heaven, has given me all the kingdoms of the earth and he has appointed me to build a temple for him at Jerusalem in Judah. 3 Any of his people among you may go up to Jerusalem in Judah and build the temple of the Lord, the God of Israel, the God who is in Jerusalem, and may their God be with them. 4 And in any locality where survivors may now be living, the people are to provide them with silver and gold, with goods and livestock, and with freewill offerings for the temple of God in Jerusalem.'"
5 Then the family heads of Judah and Benjamin, and the priests and Levites—everyone whose heart God had moved—prepared to go up and build the house of the Lord in Jerusalem.

Ezra 1-6 records the return of the first Jewish exiles, led by Zerubbabel as governor and Joshua as high priest. The people quickly began reconstructing from the rubble of the old Jerusalem an altar, and then the foundation for a new temple. But the neighboring Samaritans saw the rise of Jerusalem as a threat to their power, so they discouraged the workers, and for sixteen years, the temple was nothing but an unfinished foundation. The Jews became apathetic, fearful of their enemies and distracted by the "daily grind" of taking care of their own homes and crops. That is until Haggai came to shake things up.

Ezra 5:1-2 (NIV)

Now Haggai the prophet and Zechariah the prophet, a descendant of Iddo, prophesied to the Jews in Judah and Jerusalem in the name of the God of Israel, who was over them. 2 Then Zerubbabel son of Shealtiel and Joshua son of Jozadak set to work to rebuild the house of God in Jerusalem. And the prophets of God were with them, supporting them.

God hates paneling

Haggai 1:1-11 (NIV)

In the second year of King Darius, on the first day of the sixth month, the word of the Lord came through the prophet Haggai to Zerubbabel son of Shealtiel, governor of Judah, and to Joshua son of Jehozadak, the high priest:
2 This is what the Lord Almighty says: "These people say, 'The time has not yet come for the Lord's house to be built.'"
3 Then the word of the Lord came through the prophet Haggai: 4 "Is it a time for you yourselves to be living in your paneled houses, while this house remains a ruin?"
5 Now this is what the Lord Almighty says: "Give careful thought to your ways. 6 You have planted much, but have harvested little. You eat, but never have enough. You drink, but never have your fill. You put on clothes, but are not warm. You earn wages, only to put them in a purse with holes in it."
7 This is what the Lord Almighty says: "Give careful thought to your ways. 8 Go up into the mountains and bring down timber and build the house, so that I may take pleasure in it and be honored," says the Lord. 9 "You expected much, but see, it turned out to be little. What you brought home, I blew away. Why?" declares the Lord Almighty. "Because of my house, which remains a ruin, while each of you is busy with his own house. 10 Therefore, because of you the heavens have withheld their dew

and the earth its crops. [11] *I called for a drought on the fields and the mountains, on the grain, the new wine, the oil and whatever the ground produces, on men and cattle, and on the labor of your hands."*

"Give careful thought to your ways" in verse 7 may be calling the people's attention to the parallels between their current situation and the curses for disobedience Moses pronounced back in Deuteronomy. God wanted them to see the connection so that they understood the cause of their struggles. Compare the following curses to what we just read in Haggai 1.

Deuteronomy 28:38-39 (NIV)
[38] *You will sow much seed in the field but you will harvest little, because locusts will devour it.* [39] *You will plant vineyards and cultivate them but you will not drink the wine or gather the grapes, because worms will eat them.*

Deuteronomy 28:22-24 (NIV)
[22] *The Lord will strike you with wasting disease, with fever and inflammation, with scorching heat and drought, with blight and mildew, which will plague you until you perish.* [23] *The sky over your head will be bronze, the ground beneath you iron.* [24] *The Lord will turn the rain of your country into dust and powder; it will come down from the skies until you are destroyed.*

Group Discussion: The people apparently had been telling themselves that the time was not right to rebuild the Temple because they didn't feel financially or physically secure themselves. What did they get wrong with that philosophy?

- God says they have it backward. Things are not good and they don't feel secure because they have not been investing in their relationship with Him. Get right with the Blesser, and then blessings will follow. Instead, they wanted blessings first before getting right with God.
- *A paneled house* implies that they had been investing in the comforts and status of their homes and were not as poor as they made out to be. We tend to be more generous to ourselves than others, and it can be difficult to decide when we have enough because it is easy to convince ourselves that enough is just a little bit more.

Group Discussion: We no longer worship in a central temple; in the Christian age, congregations can and do meet in homes, in schools, and even outside under trees. So would God say the same things to us if he compared our homes to our church building? Is it fair to make this apply to our modern context?

- In the name of "good stewardship" we donate used, half-broken toys to our church's nursery after buying new toys for our kids; we stick ragged furniture in church classrooms that we would never tolerate in our own homes; we park our new cars next to the creaky old church van. What is "good enough" for church is what is not good enough for us.
- Some defend this so that outsiders will not see us as extravagant or selfish because we spent money on an attractive building instead of an orphanage. But could that argument not also have been used in Haggai's time to excuse the condition of the temple? They already had an altar and were offering sacrifices; they were covering the basics. Yet God was still not pleased. Why not?
- Even if we don't see a direct correlation between the old temple and modern church buildings, there is still an underlying principle here that is applicable: we generally make time for what is truly important to us. Why was it time to work on their houses but not on God's house? Remember that the temple signified or embodied the Lord's presence among His people. In building for themselves but not for him, the people apparently didn't mind whether the Lord lived among them or not. Their priorities were revealed by their attitude and how they spent their time and money (Carson, *New Bible Commentary*). The issue is not that they had nice homes, but that they put themselves before God.

<u>Group Discussion:</u> The Israelites had obviously achieved some degree of wealth because they lived in "paneled houses," yet they always seemed to be lacking or needing. Why did they feel like they were struggling so hard?

- God foiled their efforts so that they "planted much but harvested little" so that they would return to Him. To amass what they did, then, meant that they had to work that much harder. There was no contentment in their paneled houses. It is hard to be content when you don't feel you are getting what you deserve. They were working too hard for too little.
- There might also be a lack of contentment here that has little relationship to their possessions. After all, it does say they have houses, food, drink, clothing, and wages. They have the essentials of life, but feel empty and want more.
- They are in danger of repeating the greedy mistakes of their forefathers. In Leviticus 25, God commanded that every seventh year was to be a Sabbath year for the land. The people were to let their land and vineyards lay fallow so the soil could rest. This was a good practice ecologically, but it also forced the people to rely on God every seventh year to provide for them.

o **Leviticus 25:1-7 (NIV)** *The Lord said to Moses at Mount Sinai, [2] "Speak to the Israelites and say to them: 'When you enter the land I am going to give you, the land itself must observe a sabbath to the Lord. [3] For six years sow your fields, and for six years prune your vineyards and gather their crops. [4] But in the seventh year the land is to have a year of sabbath rest, a sabbath to the Lord. Do not sow your fields or prune your vineyards. [5] Do not reap what grows of itself or harvest the grapes of your untended vines. The land is to have a year of rest. [6] Whatever the land yields during the sabbath year will be food for you—for yourself, your male and female servants, and the hired worker and temporary resident who live among you, [7] as well as for your livestock and the wild animals in your land. Whatever the land produces may be eaten.*

- What they did, predictably, was to ignore the Sabbath year in their farming practices, and to resent the Sabbath day as an interruption to making money (Amos 8:5). They pushed and pushed for more, so that neither they nor their land had any rest. In God's eyes, this was an attempt to be so self-sufficient, so rich, that they could insulate themselves from depending on Him. This was one reason they were carried off to exile. It is one of the curses prophesied by Moses:

o **Leviticus 26:33-35 (NIV)** *[33] I will scatter you among the nations and will draw out my sword and pursue you. Your land will be laid waste, and your cities will lie in ruins. [34] Then the land will enjoy its sabbath years all the time that it lies desolate and you are in the country of your enemies; then the land will rest and enjoy its sabbaths. [35] All the time that it lies desolate, the land will have the rest it did not have during the sabbaths you lived in it.*

- And this was how the exile was summarized in Chronicles:

o **2 Chronicles 36:20-21** (NIV) *[20] He carried into exile to Babylon the remnant, who escaped from the sword, and they became servants to him and his successors until the kingdom of Persia came to power. [21] The land enjoyed its sabbath rests; all the time of its desolation it rested, until the seventy years were completed in fulfillment of the word of the LORD spoken by Jeremiah.*

<u>Group Discussion:</u> Why is it hard to find contentment without God?

- When you are not depending on God, that means you have to depend on yourself for everything. You are worried about losing what you have because it is up to you to replace it. If you don't believe God will come through, then you have to come through for yourself all the time, and that means you are motivated by fear, not trust.

God loves construction zones

Haggai 2:1-9 (NIV)

On the twenty-first day of the seventh month, the word of the Lord came through the prophet Haggai: [2] "Speak to Zerubbabel son of Shealtiel, governor of Judah, to Joshua son of Jehozadak, the high priest, and to the remnant of the people. Ask them, [3] 'Who of you is left who saw this house in its former glory? How does it look to you now? Does it not seem to you like nothing? [4] But now be strong, O Zerubbabel,' declares the Lord. 'Be strong, O Joshua son of Jehozadak, the high priest. Be strong, all you people of the land,' declares the Lord, 'and work. For I am with you,' declares the Lord Almighty. [5] 'This is what I covenanted with you when you came out of Egypt. And my Spirit remains among you. Do not fear.'
[6] "This is what the Lord Almighty says: 'In a little while I will once more shake the heavens and the earth, the sea and the dry land. [7] I will shake all nations, and the desired of all nations will come, and I will fill this house with glory,' says the Lord Almighty. [8] 'The silver is mine and the gold is mine,' declares the Lord Almighty. [9] 'The glory of this present house will be greater than the glory of the former house,' says the Lord Almighty. 'And in this place I will grant peace,' declares the Lord Almighty."

The timing of this second message is significant. The Day of Atonement and the Feast of Booths had brought many people to the Temple. As they took part in these religious observances, they were probably disappointed in how much work is left to do. Sixteen years before, when the work had first begun on the new temple, the older exiles saw the same thing:

Ezra 3:12-13 (NIV)

[12] But many of the older priests and Levites and family heads, who had seen the former temple, wept aloud when they saw the foundation of this temple being laid, while many others shouted for joy. [13] No one could distinguish the sound of the shouts of joy from the sound of weeping, because the people made so much noise. And the sound was heard far away.

<u>Group Discussion:</u> Sixteen years later, when work starts again, the results so far are less than impressive. Earlier, the people had been content with an unfinished foundation, but God was not. That's the norm – God calling His people to a higher standard, to not be content with mediocrity. Now, ironically, the temple is actually going up but the people are dissatisfied with it because it is not good enough. So why is God happy with it?

- Zechariah 4:10 (NCV) "The people should not think that small beginnings are unimportant. They will be happy when they see Zerubbabel with tools, building the Temple. "(These are the seven eyes of the Lord, which look back and forth across the earth.)"
- What happened inside that original Temple became superficial rituals by uncommitted people. The Temple had become simply hard stones housing hard hearts. Now there is just a construction zone, but it is filled with committed people purified by their experience in exile. God is reclaiming His vision for His people and His temple.
- God was no doubt pleased to see His people united in a common work. Previously they were taking care of their own houses and their own needs. Now they are united in a better cause.

<u>Group Discussion:</u> What might He mean when God says in verse 8 "the silver is mine and the gold is mine?" Why is that significant in this "pep talk" He gives to His people?

- Perhaps it is just a reminder that He can provide whatever is necessary for the temple's construction. We read later in Ezra (Ezra 6:6-12) and Nehemiah how the Persian emperors sent significant amounts of money and materials to help reconstruct Jerusalem.
- Perhaps He is reiterating that all the material "stuff" that composed the old temple is already His. What it lacked, and what He most wants to possess is the hearts of His people. Their dedication will be the real glory of this new temple.

Haggai 2:15-19 (NIV)
[15] "Now give careful thought to this from this day on—consider how things were before one stone was laid on another in the Lord's temple. [16] When anyone came to a heap of twenty measures, there were only ten. When anyone went to a wine vat to draw fifty measures, there were only twenty. [17] I struck all the work of your hands with blight, mildew and hail, yet you did not turn to me,' declares the Lord. [18] 'From this day on, from this twenty-fourth day of the ninth month, give careful thought to the day when the foundation of the Lord's temple was laid. Give careful thought: [19] Is there yet any seed left in the barn? Until now, the vine and the fig tree, the pomegranate and the olive tree have not borne fruit. "From this day on I will bless you."'

This prophecy was given on December 18, 520 BC. Winter crops were about to be planted, but there was little in storage from the meager harvests of the summer and fall. Grapes, figs and pomegranates ripened in August and September, and olives from September to November. These crops had produced poorly. But from this day on, God promises, the people will see a marked difference.

Zecheriah 8:9-13 mentions this red-letter day as well because things did get better economically once the cornerstone of the temple was laid. God made sure that connection was clear to them so there would be no misunderstanding about the source of true security and contentment. Just like God made the connection between the curses in Deuteronomy 28 with their current struggles, He wanted to make clear the connection between the completion of the Temple with a significant outpouring of future blessings.

A ring on God's finger

Haggai 2:20-23 (NIV)
[20] The word of the Lord came to Haggai a second time on the twenty-fourth day of the month: [21] 'Tell Zerubbabel governor of Judah that I will shake the heavens and the earth. [22] I will overturn royal thrones and shatter the power of the foreign kingdoms. I will overthrow chariots and their drivers; horses and their riders will fall, each by the sword of his brother.
[23] "'On that day,' declares the Lord Almighty, 'I will take you, my servant Zerubbabel son of Shealtiel,' declares the Lord, 'and I will make you like my signet ring, for I have chosen you,' declares the Lord Almighty."

A signet ring was the seal by which a king signified that something belonged to him or was under his protection. Consequently, a signet ring was something which with a king would not likely part. For God to call Zerubbabel His signet ring has an interesting background that goes back to a prophecy made by Jeremiah before the Babylonian exile:

Jeremiah 22:24-26 (NIV)
[24] "As surely as I live," declares the Lord, "even if you, Jehoiachin son of Jehoiakim king of Judah, were a signet ring on my right hand, I would still pull you off. [25] I will hand you over to those who seek your life, those you fear—to Nebuchadnezzar king of Babylon and to the Babylonians. [26] I will hurl you and the mother who gave you birth into another country, where neither of you was born, and there you both will die.

Zerubbabel, the prince of Judah who listened to Haggai and started rebuilding the temple, was the grandson of Jehoiachin. God had thrown away His grandfather to the Babylonians; now God promises Zerubbabel that He will protect and cherish him like a prized possession.

<u>Group Discussion:</u> Most congregations that plateau for even a few years never start growing again. If Haggai were a church consultant called in to work with a stagnant church, what do you think he would look for? What questions would he ask?

12
ZECHARIAH
Let's restart this relationship

Zechariah identifies himself as "son of Berekiah, the son of Iddo." There is an Iddo mentioned in Neh. 12:4, 16 who was head of a priestly family that returned from exile. If Zechariah's grandfather was this Iddo, he may have been a priest as well as a prophet. There is also this allusion to a Zechariah in Matthew:

Matthew 23:34-36 (NIV)
34 Therefore I am sending you prophets and wise men and teachers. Some of them you will kill and crucify; others you will flog in your synagogues and pursue from town to town. 35 And so upon you will come all the righteous blood that has been shed on earth, from the blood of righteous Abel to the blood of Zechariah son of Berekiah, whom you murdered between the temple and the altar. 36 I tell you the truth, all this will come upon this generation.

This may not be Zechariah the minor prophet, but another prophet mentioned in 2 Chronicles 24:20-22, who was stoned to death in the courtyard of the Temple by order of wicked king Joash. Jesus cited Abel to Zechariah perhaps as an idiom similar to our "Genesis to Revelation" because Chronicles came at the end of most Hebrew manuscripts of the Old Testament. So Jesus was citing the first murder and one of the last in the "Bible" of his time to encompass the full history of biblical people who had been killed for their righteousness.

Zechariah the minor prophet prophesied at the same time as Haggai, and was apparently a young man at that time because in a vision an angel refers to him as "this young man." He penned one of the most difficult books in the Bible. Zechariah 1-8 is unified by a common theme of restoring God's relationship with His people and rebuilding the temple.

The second half of Zechariah offers some intriguing references to the Messiah, as well as prophecies about the struggle of the Jews against Greek overlords during the inter-testamental period, the siege and destruction of Jerusalem in 70 A.D., and the final Judgment Day. Scholars have struggled with how to explain how these two halves fit together, or if they were ever intended to. They have also struggled with translating some of the Hebrew in this section. Our study will mostly stay in the first half of Zechariah to keep the length and the focus of this lesson consistent with the rest of the series.

Perhaps the most obvious theme of the book is the restoration of the exiles' relationship with God. God is convincing the Jews in Judea and throughout the Babylonian empire that He wants to "reset" their relationship with Him, as attested in verses like these:

Zechariah 1:3 (NIV)
3 Therefore tell the people: This is what the Lord Almighty says: 'Return to me,' declares the Lord Almighty, 'and I will return to you,' says the Lord Almighty.

Zechariah 10:6 (NIV)
6 "I will strengthen Judah
and save the tribes of Joseph.
I will restore them
because I have compassion on them.
They will be as though
I had not rejected them,
for I am the Lord their God
and I will answer them.

<u>Group Discussion:</u> Have you ever tried to create a fresh start in a relationship, especially one that had a contentious history, or in which someone had hurt you in the past? What was required to make that relationship work again?

I had the strangest dream . . .

To convince the people that a fresh start was possible, and that the Lord's hand had turned from punishment of them to welcoming of them, a message of reconciliation is revealed in a series of eight visions given to Zechariah all on one night, Feb. 15, 519 B.C.

These eight visions are much like what we see in Revelations, vividly cinematic, as if he had stepped into an interactive movie. We could also think of them as elaborate "skits," acted out by angels or spirit beings, to deliver divine messages from God. We will not discuss all of them, but here's a sample of one of his visions that illustrates their common theme of restoration for the Israelites and punishment on their oppressors:

Zechariah 1:8-17 (NIV)
8 During the night I had a vision, and there before me was a man mounted on a red horse. He was standing among the myrtle trees in a ravine. Behind him were red, brown and white horses.
9 I asked, "What are these, my lord?"
The angel who was talking with me answered, "I will show you what they are."
10 Then the man standing among the myrtle trees explained, "They are the ones the Lord has sent to go throughout the earth."
11 And they reported to the angel of the Lord who was standing among the myrtle trees, "We have gone throughout the earth and found the whole world at rest and in peace."
12 Then the angel of the Lord said, "Lord Almighty, how long will you withhold mercy from Jerusalem and from the towns of
Judah, which you have been angry with these seventy years?" 13 So the Lordspoke kind and comforting words to the angel who talked with me.
14 Then the angel who was speaking to me said, "Proclaim this word: This is what the Lord Almighty says: 'I am very jealous for Jerusalem and Zion, 15 and I am very angry with the nations that feel secure. I was only a little angry, but they went too far with the punishment.'
16 "Therefore this is what the Lord says: 'I will return to Jerusalem with mercy, and there my house will be rebuilt. And the measuring line will be stretched out over Jerusalem,' declares the Lord Almighty.
17 "Proclaim further: This is what the Lord Almighty says: 'My towns will again overflow with prosperity, and the Lord will again comfort Zion and choose Jerusalem.'"

<u>Group Discussion:</u> Why might God have chosen visions like this to communicate with His people?

- Visual illustrations are much more engaging than simply telling the Israelites "I am going to restore Jerusalem and destroy its enemies," or "stop lying and stealing." Stories and pictures get an audience's attention like nothing else can.
- Perhaps these visions emphasize that there is a "real" spiritual world. These images are much richer than the fluffy clouds and plinking harps of the stereotypical "heaven." These visions express in concrete, human terms the urgency, the violence, the passion with which God fights for His people and rules the universe.

One of the themes of Zechariah is that God will bring justice on the pagan nations that plundered and destroyed Judah. Even though they did so as punishment against Judah as an act of God, God also promised that those nations too – Babylon, Assyria, Persia - would be punished for their wickedness.

God also makes an interesting statement in 1:15, "*and I am very angry with the nations that feel secure. I was only a little angry, but they went too far with the punishment."*

<u>Group Discussion:</u> We get the sense that the people God sent to punish the Israelites went far beyond what they were supposed to do, as if God was not able to control them. How do you explain this verse and what it says about how God used pagan nations as His tools?

- Perhaps "a little angry" is meant to contrast God's anger with that of the Babylonians and Assyrians. This does not mean that God was not angry, but that His anger was just, righteous, and controlled. The invading nations, however, were ruthless and greedy as they swarmed over Israel. These nations, "gave help for evil" (Hebrew) or "combined to attack for evil" (Septuagint). While their actions helped fulfill God's will, their motivations were certainly not the same as God's.

Here's another of Zechariah's visions. Listen to this description of wickedness in Zechariah's seventh vision:

Zechariah 5:5-11 (NIV)

5 Then the angel who was speaking to me came forward and said to me, "Look up and see what this is that is appearing."
6 I asked, "What is it?"
He replied, "It is a measuring basket." And he added, "This is the iniquity of the people throughout the land."
7 Then the cover of lead was raised, and there in the basket sat a woman! 8 He said, "This is wickedness," and he pushed her back into the basket and pushed the lead cover down over its mouth.
9 Then I looked up—and there before me were two women, with the wind in their wings! They had wings like those of a stork, and they lifted up the basket between heaven and earth.
10 "Where are they taking the basket?" I asked the angel who was speaking to me.
11 He replied, "To the country of Babylonia to build a house for it. When it is ready, the basket will be set there in its place."

<u>Group Discussion:</u> What do we learn about the nature of wickedness in this picture/story?

- It must be treated seriously. The angels put a lead cover on it, and no sooner is the lid raised then she (wickedness) tries to get out. Zechariah's vision is reminiscent of Pandora's Box: our curiosity about wickedness can unwittingly unleash it. We need to have a faith that takes God at His word about sin – our faith needs to be stronger than our curiosity about what is under the lid.
- The way iniquity is carried from Judah to Babylon again confirms that God has carried away the history of rebellion that led to the exile, and now He wants a fresh start with His people.

Not by might or power, but by the Spirit

The rebuilding of the Temple is key in this process of restoration as a symbol of that restoration, so Zechariah intently urges its completion. It seems like a daunting task, but the prophet reminds them that they are not doing this alone.

Zechariah 4:6-9 (NIV)
6 So he said to me, "This is the word of the Lord to Zerubbabel: 'Not by might nor by power, but by my Spirit,' says the Lord Almighty.
7 "What are you, mighty mountain? Before Zerubbabel you will become level ground. Then he will bring out the capstone to shouts of 'God bless it! God bless it!'"
8 Then the word of the Lord came to me: 9 "The hands of Zerubbabel have laid the foundation of this temple; his hands will also complete it. Then you will know that the Lord Almighty has sent me to you.

Zechariah 8:7-13 (NIV)
7 This is what the Lord Almighty says: "I will save my people from the countries of the east and the west. 8 I will bring them back to live in Jerusalem; they will be my people, and I will be faithful and righteous to them as their God."
9 This is what the Lord Almighty says: "Now hear these words, 'Let your hands be strong so that the temple may be built.' This is also what the prophets said who were present when the foundation was laid for the house of the Lord Almighty. 10 Before that time there were no wages for people or hire for animals. No one could go about their business safely because of their enemies, since I had turned everyone against their neighbor. 11 But now I will not deal with the remnant of this people as I did in the past," declares the Lord Almighty.
12 "The seed will grow well, the vine will yield its fruit, the ground will produce its crops, and the heavens will drop their dew. I will give all these things as an inheritance to the remnant of this people. 13 Just as you, Judah and Israel, have been a curse among the nations, so I will save you, and you will be a blessing. Do not be afraid, but let your hands be strong."

<u>Group Discussion:</u> In these passages, what has or will God do to see the Temple completed? What is God's role? What is the role of the people?

- God has given them rest from their enemies and neutralized foreign threats.
- He has made it possible for the exiles to return to Jerusalem from where they have been scattered.
- He has promised that the same governor (Zerubbabel) who started the project will see it to completion.
- He has promised prosperity so the people are not working under financial difficulty.
- For the people's part, they just need to believe what God has already promised and put their hand to the work.

Was it really for me?

Zechariah 7:1-6 (NIV)
In the fourth year of King Darius, the word of the Lord came to Zechariah on the fourth day of the ninth month, the month of Kislev. 2 The people of Bethel had sent Sharezer and Regem-Melech, together with their men, to entreat the Lord 3 by asking the priests of the house of the Lord Almighty and the prophets, "Should I mourn and fast in the fifth month, as I have done for so many years?"
4 Then the word of the Lord Almighty came to me: 5 "Ask all the people of the land and the priests, 'When you fasted and mourned in the fifth and seventh months for the past seventy years, was it really for me that you fasted? 6 And when you were eating and drinking, were you not just feasting for yourselves?

The festival cycle that God instituted for the Jews is outlined in Leviticus 23. Fasting was only commanded on one of those, the Day of Atonement. After the exile, the Jews added several other days of fasting and memorial to their calendar. Zechariah 8:19 mentions fasts practiced by the exiles on the fourth, fifth, seventh and tenth month of the Jewish year (Arthur 59-60).

1) A day of fasting and mourning in the fifth month was in remembrance of the destruction of the temple in 586 B.C. (2 Kings 25:9).
2) A day of fasting in the seventh month was in remembrance of the murder of Gedaliah, who had been appointed governor by the Babylonians (2 Kings 25:22-25).
3) The fast on the fourth month commemorated Jerusalem's defeat by Nebuchadnezzar recorded in 2 Kings 25:3-4.
4) The fast on the tenth month commemorated the beginning of the siege of Jerusalem (2 Kings 25:1).

Group Discussion: Why would God respond so sarcastically to this question from the people of Bethel? Isn't fasting and humility what He would have appreciated among His people?

- This apparently goes back to the attitude problem among the Israelites even before the exile. They tried to pile on even more religious activity to please God instead of making the hard choices that reflected a change of heart. These acts of piety were just that – acting. Fasting made the people *feel* religious, but that feeling did not change their lifestyles or attitudes.
- Notice too that all these fasts commemorated defeats that were God's will. They were sorry for themselves and what they had lost. They longed for the old Jerusalem, but the old Jerusalem had been so corrupt God destroyed it. To now long for what they had left behind was to disrespect God's will and to show a lack of appreciation for how He blessed them as exiles.

Zechariah's answer to this question about days of fasting actually continues over several paragraphs from 7:4 – 8:19. The final answer is in 8:18-19:

Zechariah 8:18-19 (NIV)
18 Again the word of the Lord Almighty came to me. 19 This is what the Lord Almighty says: "The fasts of the fourth, fifth, seventh and tenth months will become joyful and glad occasions and happy festivals for Judah. Therefore love truth and peace."

But here's what you can do for me . . .

God's short answer is there is no reason to continue these days of fasting; they are fasting for selfish reasons and for sorrows that have now been turned to joy, so there is no reason to be fasting. The full answer, though, is that while they should not be fasting, He does expect them to do something else instead, and He repeats the same instructions twice for emphasis:

Zechariah 7:8-10 (NIV)
8 And the word of the Lord came again to Zechariah: 9 "This is what the Lord Almighty says: 'Administer true justice; show mercy and compassion to one another. 10 Do not oppress the widow or the fatherless, the alien or the poor. In your hearts do not think evil of each other.'

Zechariah 8:16-17 (NIV)
16 These are the things you are to do: Speak the truth to each other, and render true and sound judgment in your courts; 17 do not plot evil against your neighbor, and do not love to swear falsely. I hate all this," declares the Lord.

<u>Group Discussion:</u> Why would God want these things from His people instead of special days of fasting and mourning?

- God is more concerned with how we live our "everyday" days versus special days. Our weekdays and workdays carry more weight than our holy days. Occasional fasts and acts of piety do not cover over a week or month of hard selfishness.
- Religious people tend to get fixated on the fine points, the tangents, the trivia of religion, and wholly miss the very purpose of their religion. The people of Bethel ask about a few days of fasting, acts never required or mentioned by God, while missing completely what God *has* commanded of them – compassion, mercy, truth, and justice – the very basics of just being decent humans. It is much easier to discuss trivia because that doesn't require us to change how we live; if it does require a change, that change is just some fine tuning within our religious "compartment," which usually is relegated to a few hours a week and does not ruin what we *really* want to do anyway.
- The reason God hauled off his people to exile, the reason that upon returning to exile they still lived dreary and unfulfilling lives, is that they ignored the heart of the Law: love God and love your neighbor as yourself.

Here is the man whose name is The Branch

The frequent messianic prophecies in Zechariah fit with its theme of restoration. Jesus is the priest and king who will make possible the perfect spiritual reunion of God and all people by forgiving sin and conquering death. It is outside the scope of this study to explore that topic in depth, but here is a sampling of those messianic prophecies. We'll read the prophecy from Zechariah first, and then see if you can explain how that is fulfilled in Christ, after which we'll give New Testament fulfillments or quotes of that prophetic verse.

Zechariah 6:12-13 (NIV)

12 Tell him this is what the Lord Almighty says: 'Here is the man whose name is the Branch, and he will branch out from his place and build the temple of the Lord. 13 It is he who will build the temple of the Lord, and he will be clothed with majesty and will sit and rule on his throne. And he will be a priest on his throne. And there will be harmony between the two.'

<u>Group Discussion:</u> How does that connect to Jesus, or how is that fulfilled in Jesus?

- The Branch is a messianic reference based in Isaiah 11, which promises the messiah will be a branch or offspring of Jesse (father of King David).
- In John 3:19-22, Jesus refers to his body as the temple.
- Compare Zechariah 6:12 to John 19:5, where Pilate introduces Jesus with "Here is the man!"
- Also compare it to John 19:14, "'Here is your king,' Pilate said to the Jews."

Zechariah 9:9 (NIV)

9 Rejoice greatly, Daughter Zion!
Shout, Daughter Jerusalem!
See, your king comes to you,
righteous and victorious,
lowly and riding on a donkey,
on a colt, the foal of a donkey.

<u>Group Discussion:</u> How does that connect to Jesus, or how is that fulfilled in Jesus?

- Jesus rode on a donkey with a colt as he triumphantly entered Jerusalem in Matthew 21:5.

Zechariah 9:10 (NIV)

10 *I will take away the chariots from Ephraim*
and the warhorses from Jerusalem,
and the battle bow will be broken.
He will proclaim peace to the nations.
His rule will extend from sea to sea
and from the River to the ends of the earth.

<u>Group Discussion:</u> How does that connect to Jesus, or how is that fulfilled in Jesus?

- In Matthew 28:19, Jesus commissions his disciples to go and make disciples of all nations.
- In Acts 1:8, he says his disciples "will be my witnesses . . . to the ends of the earth."

Zechariah 12:10 (NIV)

10 *"And I will pour out on the house of David and the inhabitants of Jerusalem a spirit of grace and supplication. They will look on me, the one they have pierced, and they will mourn for him as one mourns for an only child, and grieve bitterly for him as one grieves for a firstborn son.*

<u>Group Discussion:</u> How does that connect to Jesus, or how is that fulfilled in Jesus?

- In John 19:34, a Roman soldier pierces Jesus' side to ensure he is dead, and this verse in Zechariah is recalled by John in John 19:37.

Zechariah 13:7 (NIV)

7 *"Awake, sword, against my shepherd,*
against the man who is close to me!"
declares the Lord Almighty.
"Strike the shepherd,
and the sheep will be scattered,
and I will turn my hand against the little ones.

<u>Group Discussion:</u> How does that connect to Jesus, or how is that fulfilled in Jesus?

- Jesus quotes that verse in Matthew 26:31, predicting what will happen when he is arrested in Matthew 26:56.

Zechariah 13:1 (NIV)

"On that day a fountain will be opened to the house of David and the inhabitants of Jerusalem, to cleanse them from sin and impurity.

<u>Group Discussion:</u> How does that connect to Jesus, or how is that fulfilled in Jesus?

- In Matthew 26:28, Jesus teaches how his blood is poured out (like a fountain) for the forgiveness of sins.

13
MALACHI
I have always loved you

Malachi preaches to disillusioned Jewish exiles who are asking if this is as good as it gets. The temple that Haggai and Zechariah had persuaded Zerubbabel to finish was now done. However, the fulfillment of prophecies about what would come with the restoration of the Temple had not come to fruition. The wonderful era of prosperity and influence the exiles expected was not evident. The priestly king they had been awaiting had not yet appeared. Malachi 3:1 implies that there had been no supernatural events, no miracles in the Temple, unlike when Solomon dedicated his Temple (2 Chronicles 7:1-3).

This era is marked by cynicism, skepticism, disillusionment, and lethargy. Judea is a minor province of the Persian empire, about 20 miles by 30 miles in area, with no army and for many years no walls around its capitol city of Jerusalem.

Perhaps because of their defeated hearts and vulnerable position, Malachi, more than any other Old Testament book, uses "Lord of Hosts" or "Lord of Heaven's Army" (New Century translation) as a title for God to remind them that they do have security and an "army" in God their Protector.

God had sent the prophets Haggai and Zechariah to support the work of governor Zerubbabel in rebuilding the Temple. They had brought fresh fire to a renewed vision for a discouraged people. Now, approximately 70 years later, God sends the prophet Malachi to again bring fresh fire and vision in support of Nehemiah rebuilding the wall of Jerusalem and the practices within the Temple.

God puts the people's discontent and cynicism on trial in Malachi, and forces them to examine the false assumptions on which they justify their lethargy. The structure of Malachi suggests a courtroom drama, with God as prosecutor and judge. God makes an accusation, such as "It is you, O priests, who show contempt for my name." Then He anticipates how the people would question that statement: "But you ask, 'How have we shown contempt for your name?'" Then He answers their objections or questions with evidence from the practices and actions of the people: "You place defiled food on my altar."

The issues addressed by Malachi were some of the same issues addressed by Ezra and Nehemiah as they attempted to revive God's vision for the exiles when they rebuilt the wall around Jerusalem. For this reason, most scholars date Malachi to the period prior to or during the lifetimes of Ezra and Nehemiah, or perhaps in the 12-year absence of Nehemiah from Jerusalem after rebuilding the wall (Nehemiah 13:6). This means Malachi was most likely the last prophet of the Old Testament era, writing sometime after the temple was completed in 516 B.C. and before 433 B.C. when Nehemiah returned to Jerusalem.

The headings for each section of this lesson reflect the major indictments delivered by God in the "courtroom drama" of Malachi.

Indictment #1: I have always loved you

Malachi 1:1-5 (NIV)

An oracle: The word of the Lord to Israel through Malachi.
2 "I have loved you," says the Lord.
"But you ask, 'How have you loved us?'
"Was not Esau Jacob's brother?" the Lord says. "Yet I have loved Jacob, 3 but Esau I have hated, and I have turned his mountains into a wasteland and left his inheritance to the desert jackals."
4 Edom may say, "Though we have been crushed, we will rebuild the ruins."
But this is what the Lord Almighty says: "They may build, but I will demolish. They will be called the Wicked Land, a people always under the wrath of the Lord.
5 You will see it with your own eyes and say, 'Great is the Lord—even beyond the borders of Israel!'

Group Discussion: Strangely, God proves His love for Israel by pointing out how He hates their "cousins" the Edomites. Why would God say this? What proof would that be for the Israelites?

- The love/hate language used by God to describe His choice of Jacob and His rejection of Esau should be understood as covenant language. God chose the Israelites as the original beneficiaries of His covenant. God Himself told His people not to despise the Edomites (Deut. 23:7-8) and that the Edomites could enter the assembly of the Lord like the rest of the Israelites after a specified time (Deut. 23:8). God does not hate Edom in the sense we understand that word. Hate is to be understood as the contrast created by His choice of one group of people over another to carry on the story of Him relating to humankind (Morgan 59). It is an idiom meant to highlight a contrast, with *love* referring to a choice and *hate* referring to rejection (ESV footnote on Malachi 1:2).
- Nonetheless, the Edomites were often the target of threatening prophecies because of their arrogance. They had already been chased out of their mountainous homeland by the Nabateans. The Edomites were already subdued and would entirely disappear as a people within a few centuries. The Israelites could look south and see the devastated condition of the nation of Edom compared to their own status. Even though things were not all rosy in the Promised Land, at least Israel had returned from exile, rebuilt the temple, and had a dialogue with God through the prophet Malachi.

Group Discussion: Throughout the prophets, God constantly reminds the Israelites that they were *chosen*. To just be God's people had intrinsic rewards that they took for granted or ignored. Do you realize that as a Christian *you* are chosen by God (see verses below)? What are some intrinsic rewards of being God's "chosen" that Christians tend to take for granted?

- **Romans 11:5-6** (NIV) 5 So too, at the present time there is a remnant chosen by grace. 6 And if by grace, then it is no longer by works; if it were, grace would no longer be grace.
- **1 Thessalonians 1:2-4** (NIV) 2 We always thank God for all of you, mentioning you in our prayers. 3 We continually remember before our God and Father your work produced by faith, your labor prompted by love, and your endurance inspired by hope in our Lord Jesus Christ. 4 For we know, brothers loved by God, that he has chosen you,
- **Ephesians 1:4-9** (NIV) 4 For he chose us in him before the creation of the world to be holy and blameless in his sight. In love 5 he predestined us to be adopted as his sons through Jesus Christ, in accordance with his pleasure and will— 6 to the praise of his glorious grace, which he has freely given us in the One he loves. 7 In him we have redemption through his blood, the forgiveness of sins, in accordance with the riches of God's grace 8 that he lavished on us with all wisdom and understanding. 9 And he made known to us the mystery of his will according to his good pleasure, which he purposed in Christ . . .

Indictment #2: Where are the honor and respect I deserve?

Malachi 1:6-14 (NIV)
6 "A son honors his father, and a servant his master. If I am a father, where is the honor due me? If I am a master, where is the respect due me?" says the Lord Almighty. "It is you, O priests, who show contempt for my name.
"But you ask, 'How have we shown contempt for your name?'
7 "You place defiled food on my altar.
"But you ask, 'How have we defiled you?'
"By saying that the Lord's table is contemptible. 8 When you bring blind animals for sacrifice, is that not wrong? When you sacrifice crippled or diseased animals, is that not wrong? Try offering them to your governor! Would he be pleased with you? Would he accept you?" says the Lord Almighty.
9 "Now implore God to be gracious to us. With such offerings from your hands, will he accept you?"—says the Lord Almighty.
10 "Oh, that one of you would shut the temple doors, so that you would not light useless fires on my altar! I am not pleased with you," says the Lord Almighty, "and I will accept no offering from your hands. 11 My name will be great among the nations, from the rising to the setting of the sun. In every place incense and pure offerings will be brought to my name, because my name will be great among the nations," says the Lord Almighty.
12 "But you profane it by saying of the Lord's table, 'It is defiled,' and of its food, 'It is contemptible.' 13 And you say, 'What a burden!' and you sniff at it contemptuously," says the Lord Almighty.
"When you bring injured, crippled or diseased animals and offer them as sacrifices, should I accept them from your hands?" says the Lord. 14 "Cursed is the cheat who has an acceptable male in his flock and vows to give it, but then sacrifices a blemished animal to the Lord. For I am a great king," says the Lord Almighty, "and my name is to be feared among the nations.

<u>Group Discussion:</u> What is wrong with the sacrifices the people are bringing to the priests?

- **Deuteronomy 15:21 (NIV)** 21 If an animal has a defect, is lame or blind, or has any serious flaw, you must not sacrifice it to the Lord your God.
- The principle behind the sacrifices offered to God was that the people were to bring their first and their best. God made concessions for the poor people who could not afford even the standard sacrifices, but everyone was to sacrifice something.
- By giving lame, crippled, reject animals, the people were not only disobeying God, but emptying the sacrifices of their purpose entirely. They were giving token leftovers while keeping the best for themselves. This showed no respect, no trust, no hope in God. This is why God says in verse 10 He wishes someone would just shut the temple doors so they stop wasting their energy on these "useless fires." The sacrifices have degenerated into insulting charades.

<u>Group Discussion:</u> Why are the priests allowing this? Why are they offering these token, blemished sacrifices anyway?

- Obviously part of the problem is just plain laziness. It is easiest to just let the people bring token gifts and show up for some rituals that makes them feel religious without making any real sacrifices.
- The priests may also have been timid because they felt dependant on the goodwill of the people. Since their compensation is eating a portion of the sacrifices, they are now left to eating mangy, diseased animals. We'll read later in 2:9 that the priests are "despised and humiliated before all the people" because of their laziness and lack of self-respect.
- As we said earlier, vision leaks, and the vision of the priests has gone entirely flat. They no longer think about why they are doing what they are doing. They find their duties tiresome (1:13) and the rewards few.

In contrast to the indifferent attitude and blasphemous actions of the postexilic priests, Yahweh announces a future day when he would be honored worldwide. "For from the rising of the sun even unto the going down of the same my name shall be great among the Gentiles." Some think that the context demands a present rather than a future tense. In this case the reference would be to the Jews who were scattered among the Gentiles in Malachi's day. More likely this is a prophecy of the conversion of the Gentiles in the days of Messiah. Among those Gentiles God's name would be "great," i.e., treated with the utmost respect. Under the Mosaic system any offering made apart from the Temple was illegal and unclean. Yet this prophecy announces that all over the world such sacrifice would be offered by sincere worshipers and accepted by a holy God. The implication is that the Mosaic system would be replaced by a new worship system. In that day Gentiles would be included among the people of God. (Smith, Malachi 1:11)

Group Discussion: Why does God end this section with "my name is to be feared among the nations?" What is the connection between what the priests were or were not doing and the image of God as a great king to be feared?

- They were making token, convenient sacrifices totally disproportionate to the greatness of the LORD Almighty. They would never insult their governor with the half-hearted effort and measly gifts they are giving to the King of kings.
- In the eyes of others, small gifts and puny efforts were understood to mean that the Israelites' must have a small, puny God.

Group Discussion: To be fair, for these priests, worship was a *duty*. They probably did not wake up every morning of their lives overjoyed that yet again they had to spend all day up to their elbows in blood, immersed in the smell of burning flesh and animal manure. We are not in a temple, we do not offer animal sacrifices, but do you see in this warning from Malachi to the priests any applications to our worship, our offerings, or our service to God?

- Worship is not just about showing up. Nor should we resign ourselves to shallow, unorganized, or dull worship experiences every week because we are just giving God the required hour or two a week. We are called to excellence, not mediocrity. Yet just like those priests who probably did not feel very thankful or worshipful every morning, we need to continue showing up, week after week, trusting that God will smile on our simple obedience.
- Have we fostered a culture of token sacrifices? Have we adjusted our expectations of church membership and involvement according to what is convenient for us or what is glorious to God? Do we just shrug when volunteer teachers come ten minutes late to a children's class if they come at all? Is the quality of work and commitment we give to our jobs far better than what we are willing to give to the church's ministries? Is there any *real* sacrifice required of us in our church in terms of money or time?
- Do we relegate castoffs to the church that we ourselves would not tolerate? For example, do we "donate" to the church things like dilapidated furniture that we would never use in our own homes?
- How do our efforts, commitment, and gifts appear to others? Does our Christianity reflect that we are servants of a great King? Does our example of faith encourage a sense of respect for God among outsiders? We can't lead others where we ourselves refuse to go, be it with sacrifice or investment or study.

Indictment #3: Being unfaithful to your wife is being unfaithful to Me

Malachi 2:10-16 (NIV)
[10] Do we not all have one Father? Did not one God create us? Why do we profane the covenant of our ancestors by being unfaithful to one another?
[11] Judah has been unfaithful. A detestable thing has been committed in Israel and in Jerusalem: Judah has desecrated the sanctuary the Lord loves by marrying women who worship a foreign god. [12] As for the man who does this, whoever he may be, may the Lord remove him from the tents of Jacob[f]—even though he brings an offering to the Lord Almighty.
[13] Another thing you do: You flood the Lord's altar with tears. You weep and wail because he no longer looks with favor on your offerings or accepts them with pleasure from your hands. [14] You ask, "Why?" It is because the Lord is the witness between you and the wife of your youth. You have been unfaithful to her, though she is your partner, the wife of your marriage covenant.
[15] Has not the one God made you? You belong to him in body and spirit. And what does the one God seek? Godly offspring. [g] So be on your guard, and do not be unfaithful to the wife of your youth.
[16] "The man who hates and divorces his wife," says the Lord, the God of Israel, "does violence to the one he should protect," [h] says the Lord Almighty.
So be on your guard, and do not be unfaithful.

This is a reminder that God sees marriage differently than some of us. To Him, it is a covenant between a man and a woman and God. That is why their unfaithfulness to their wives, especially when they divorce their first wives to marry pagan foreign women, is so odious to Him. Nehemiah forcefully confronted this in Nehemiah 13 by publicly shaming the Israelite men with foreign wives and children who lived as pagans.

Notice too the correlation in Malachi 2:13-16 between the effectiveness of our worship and prayers to our home life. God does not bless us when we don't bless those in our own home.

1 Peter 3:7 (NIV)
[7] Husbands, in the same way be considerate as you live with your wives, and treat them with respect as the weaker partner and as heirs with you of the gracious gift of life, so that nothing will hinder your prayers.

Indictment #4: The justice you say you desire is coming

Malachi 2:17 – 3:5 (NIV)
[17] You have wearied the Lord with your words.
"How have we wearied him?" you ask.
By saying, "All who do evil are good in the eyes of the Lord, and he is pleased with them" or "Where is the God of justice?"
"I will send my messenger, who will prepare the way before me. Then suddenly the Lord you are seeking will come to his temple; the messenger of the covenant, whom you desire, will come," says the Lord Almighty.
[2] But who can endure the day of his coming? Who can stand when he appears? For he will be like a refiner's fire or a launderer's soap. [3] He will sit as a refiner and purifier of silver; he will purify the Levites and refine them like gold and silver. Then the Lord will have men who will bring offerings in righteousness, [4] and the offerings of Judah and Jerusalem will be acceptable to the Lord, as in days gone by, as in former years.
[5] "So I will come to put you on trial. I will be quick to testify against sorcerers, adulterers and perjurers, against those who defraud laborers of their wages, who oppress the widows and the fatherless, and deprive the foreigners among you of justice, but do not fear me," says the Lord Almighty.

Group Discussion: The people say they want justice, and they are accusing God of not delivering justice. God says His justice is coming, and it will be like refiner's fire or a launderer's soap. What are those images meant to teach about His justice?

- These people complaining about the lack of justice are not realizing that they too will face the same justice, and they will not fare well.
- Intense fire was used in refining metal to burn off the dross or impurities. Soap of course is likewise meant to clean.
- This indictment is actually giving the people a choice: they can choose purification, which will be thorough and therefore painful, like fire and harsh soap, or if they reject being purified by God, then they will face judgment. Those who reject purification – people like sorcerers and adulterers and abusers who do not fear God – will face the awful judgment of God.

Group Discussion: Who is the messenger mentioned in verse 1 that will prepare the people's hearts for purification and repentance?

- Jesus quoted this verse in Matthew 11:10 and applied it to John the Baptist.

Indictment #5: You have cheated me

Malachi 3:8-12 (NIV)

8 "Will a man rob God? Yet you rob me.
"But you ask, 'How do we rob you?'
"In tithes and offerings. 9 You are under a curse—the whole nation of you—because you are robbing me. 10 Bring the whole tithe into the storehouse, that there may be food in my house. Test me in this," says the Lord Almighty, "and see if I will not throw open the floodgates of heaven and pour out so much blessing that you will not have room enough for it. 11 I will prevent pests from devouring your crops, and the vines in your fields will not cast their fruit," says the Lord Almighty. 12 "Then all the nations will call you blessed, for yours will be a delightful land," says the Lord Almighty.

Group Discussion: The NIV interprets v 10 " ***… and pour out so much blessing that you will not have room enough for it.*** **" The HCSB translation renders it "** ***. . . and pour out a blessing for you without measure.*** **" A more literal translation may be ' … and pour out for you a blessing until there is no more need' (Carson). Does that difference in translation put a different slant on this verse for you?**

We often say, collection plate in hand, that we are to "give as we have prospered." In this situation, though, the people are to give even though they have *not* prospered. Their giving will be the trigger for their prosperity. The tithe comes first, and then the blessings.

Group Discussion: "Don't test God" is a well-worn caution, yet here God encourages his people to test Him in this particular challenge. When is it okay to "test" God and when is it not?

- *Shepherd's Notes* explains the difference this way: *"Lest we conclude that God's invitation to put Him to the test is a universal principle that applies to all people at all times, we need to note that there are times when God does not encourage or condone human beings putting Him to the test. The psalmist warned against putting God to the test as the Israelites had done during the exodus (Psalm 95:8-11; also Num. 14:22-23). Jesus refused to put God to a test when Satan suggested he leap from the temple on the basis of a scriptural promise taken out of context (Matt. 4:7). To step out in faith when God invites us to test His faithfulness is a matter of obedience. To put God to the test without His invitation is a matter of presumption and sin."*

Indictment #6: You have said harsh things against me

Malachi 3:13-15 (NIV)

[13] "You have said harsh things against me," says the Lord.
"Yet you ask, 'What have we said against you?'
[14] "You have said, 'It is futile to serve God. What did we gain by carrying out his requirements and going about like mourners before the Lord Almighty? [15] But now we call the arrogant blessed. Certainly the evildoers prosper, and even those who challenge God escape.'"

These are perhaps the most damning indictments of all. What the people said or thought was not just harsh. Think about what they were saying about the nature of the holy God: God is not just or righteous; He does not bless; He does not love. What they are saying is blasphemous.

Malachi 3:13-15 echoes the same complaint heard in 2:17:

[17] You have wearied the Lord with your words.
"How have we wearied him?" you ask.
By saying, "All who do evil are good in the eyes of the Lord, and he is pleased with them" or "Where is the God of justice?"

<u>Group Discussion:</u> Why would such statements "weary" God?

- This is the sort of short-sighted complaining that all the prophets dealt with. As humans, we tend to transfer our personal feelings and circumstances to universal generalizations. If we are unhappy or hopeless or depressed, those emotions color everything we see. For instance, if we are unemployed and struggling to find another job, it doesn't matter to us how good the national unemployment rate may be, we are still 100% unemployed. We also have very narrow perspectives. What is happening to us right now tends to obliterate whatever we have experienced in the past. We don't thank God for the past 20 years when we had a good job. Our prayers are obsessed with why God doesn't seem to be helping us now. So often our spiritual question is "what have you done for me lately?"
- God's people constantly forget their history of deliverance, their status as God's chosen, and the eternal rewards waiting for them. Instead, seeing only their immediate circumstances and their immediate needs, they are way too eager to dismiss the eternal God because of temporary tests.

<u>Group Discussion:</u> So much of what the people long for will come in the figure of Jesus. So much of what they yearn to hear and see from God will be heard and seen in Jesus. Think if you lived in the time of Malachi, as one of the returned exiles. What would you find most difficult spiritually about living in this time when the prophecies about prosperity and restoration seemed unfulfilled, and the promised Messiah would not come for centuries?

ABOUT THE AUTHOR

Scott Franks has served as a minister for churches in Oklahoma and Texas. He is currently the Preaching Minister for the Burnt Hickory Church of Christ in Marietta, Georgia. Other works by Scott can be found at scottgarret.com. He also contributes to the Facebook sites 728b and Leading Churches.

Made in the USA
Coppell, TX
15 September 2023

21585314R00059